Down a Country Road

Fifty-two seasonal readings from out where the sky springs free

Eric E Wright

DayOne

© Day One Publications 2008
First printed 2008

ISBN 978-1-84625-106-1

Unless otherwise indicated, Scripture quotations in this publication are from the **New International Version** (NIV), copyright ©1973, 1978, 1984, International Bible Society. Used by permission of Hodder and Stoughton, a member of the Hodder Headline Group. All rights reserved.

British Library Cataloguing in Publication Data available

Published by Day One Publications
Ryelands Road, Leominster, HR6 8NZ
☎ 01568 613 740 FAX 01568 611 473
email—sales@dayone.co.uk
web site—www.dayone.co.uk
North American—e-mail—sales@dayonebookstore.com
North American—web site—www.dayonebookstore.com

All rights reserved
No part of this publication may be reproduced, or stored in a retrieval system, or transmitted, in any form or by any means, mechanical, electronic, photocopying, recording or otherwise, without the prior permission of Day One Publications.

Cover design by Wayne McMaster
Printed by Gutenberg Press, Malta

The sample pieces I have seen of Eric Wright's devotional book Down a Country Road reflect his sound biblical understanding and excellent writing style. My own frustration with the simple devotions published in so many booklets and one-year books has made me wish for something not only longer, but also with more depth. A book like this will go a long way to filling that void.

Ray Wiseman, biographer, columnist and speaker

I am always looking for ways to encourage and build up youth and adult volunteers. Devotional books in particular are helpful. This book is written in chapters that give a little more content than the traditional one-a-day devotional page. This makes it meatier and more fulfilling, in particular for the Christian who wants to read more than just a paragraph. This book ties in beautifully with creation. It is well written, interesting, thought-provoking, beautifully illustrated throughout with personal stories, and well worth the read.

Deborah Marling, former Director of Children's Ministries, Cobourg Alliance Church

God speaks to us in the storm, but more often in the ordinary of every day. Thankfully, Eric Wright has been listening. This book is a delightful journey down a road seldom travelled any more, a road where the simple is profound, where the extraordinary is commonplace, where the most urgent thing we need to do is stop, hear God's voice, and listen.

Phil Callaway, well-known author in Christian circles in North America

Dedication

To Mary Helen

my

country soulmate

Contents

Contents

Contents

preface

I finished writing this book just before Christmas during a particularly warm December. Christmas day ended in a driving rainstorm. Few things are more miserable than cold rain, foggy roads and soggy ground in Canada, where we're used to a white Christmas. So I was delighted when I woke the next morning to a world transformed. White, glistening snow adorned everything in sight.

Along our country road, changing scenery is the norm. Through the seasons; in the sky; down by the stream; in the woods; across the fields: everything illustrates some divine truth or reflects some characteristic of our heavenly Creator. 'Day after day they pour forth speech' (Psalm 19:2). 'For since the creation of the world God's invisible qualities—his eternal power and divine nature—have been clearly seen' (Romans 1:20).

The pages that follow contain the devotional thoughts these scenes have stimulated in my mind. They crystallize meditations on the attributes of God, sin and righteousness, salvation and Christian living, faith and works, fellowship and solitude, heaven and hell, bitterness and blessing, worship and prayer—and much more.

Devotions in this book are longer than most in this genre. I sought to follow each theme as deeply into the scriptural treasure house as I could in around three pages. They are not devotions to read every day; I'd suggest you read one a week. A Bible reading accompanies each devotion.

The prologue contains one devotion that lays out the biblical basis for discovering God's fingerprints in the created world.

Each devotion ends with a prayer that expresses many of my personal aspirations—and what I imagine yours might be. As you will soon realize, these are not words of inspiration that come from a super saint. No, they reflect the struggles of an ordinary Christian as he grapples with the challenges of following Christ Jesus in the midst of all the static thrown up by our contemporary culture.

My wife and helpmate, Mary Helen, will also appear often in these chapters. In 1991, Mary Helen and I fulfilled a dream of moving from the city to the country. Through providential circumstances, we purchased a log home an hour's drive eastwards from Toronto. It nestled beside a large tract of forest in the rolling hills of Southern Ontario. (The story of the twelve years we spent there is told in *Through a Country Window*.[1]) In

2004, health concerns dictated a simplification of our lifestyle. We couldn't bear to leave the countryside, so we moved to a smaller house in a grove of mature trees by a babbling brook.

I pray that these devotional thoughts will inspire you to celebrate the creative majesty of God in the world he has created and continues to sustain. May they also draw you closer to Jesus Christ, our Lord. I welcome any comments or questions; please contact me through Day One.

Notes

1 Eric E. Wright, *Through a Country Window* (Ontario: Essence Publishing).

Prologue: The fingerprints of God

Bible reading
Psalm 9

We drive our ingenious machines along a labyrinth of asphalt pathways to vast malls, office towers, factories and sprawling suburbs. We arrive home, where, with the click of a button, our garage doors open. Inside, we have dishwashers and microwaves, televisions and stoves, clocks and stereos. Outside, we have domesticated gardens, patios and swimming pools. Satellites orbit above us. We send probes into deep space.

We have arrived at the pinnacle of history! We are the lords of all we survey, sovereign over nature—a concept invented in the eighteenth century. We, the sophisticates of the twenty-first century, arrive in state-of-the-art hospitals and leave in elegant, gilded boxes.

Is this all there is? Absolutely not! God's providence undergirds all of life. The operation of the created universe is so dependable that we often take it for granted: the rise of the sun in the morning, the tides that sweep our oceans, the hearts that pump life through our bodies and the kidneys that expel poison from our systems. These are not the result of blind forces, nor do we exist in a serendipitous moment in almost infinite time. We have not happened upon the luck of the draw in a cosmic game of chance.

Hebrew patriarchs, psalmists and prophets knew that the reality of God as Creator and Ruler of the universe is the most foundational fact of existence. Melchizedek bore witness to this truth: 'Blessed be Abram by God Most High, Creator of heaven and earth' (Genesis 14:19). Moses sang about 'your Father, your Creator, who made you and formed you' (Deuteronomy 32:6). King David added his voice: 'The earth is the LORD's and everything in it, the world, and all who live in it; for he founded it upon the seas and established it upon the waters' (Psalm 24:1–2). Solomon exhorted young people to establish a lifelong pattern of faith in the Creator: 'Remember your Creator in the days of your youth' (Ecclesiastes 12:1).

Recognition of God's creative genius inevitably leads to a renewed faith in his wisdom and power. Often, that is just what we need. Isaiah encouraged weary Israel, 'Have you not heard? The LORD is the everlasting God, the Creator of the ends of the earth. He will not grow tired or weary, and his understanding no one can fathom. He gives strength to the weary and increases the power of the weak' (Isaiah 40:28–29).

When they were in despair, Jeremiah gave Israel hope through prophecy of a new covenant bringing forgiveness for past transgressions. He reminded the people that God's promise was as certain as the rising of the sun: 'This is what the LORD says, he who appoints the sun to shine by day, who decrees the moon and stars to shine by night, who stirs up the sea so that its waves roar—the LORD Almighty is his name' (Jeremiah 31:35).

The early Christians followed a similar pattern. Persecuted believers gathered together and prayed, 'Sovereign Lord, you made the heaven and the earth and the sea, and everything in them … enable your servants to speak your word with great boldness' (Acts 4:24,29). When pagans in Lystra wanted to sacrifice to Paul and Barnabas as if they were gods, Paul responded, 'Why are you doing this? We too are only men, human like you. We are bringing you good news, telling you to turn from these worthless things to the living God, who made heaven and earth and sea and everything in them' (Acts 14:15). In Athens, Paul declared that the 'unknown God' they worshipped ignorantly was 'The God who made the world and everything in it' (Acts 17:24).

The most important truth in the New Testament is the revelation of God's redemptive glory through the salvation of sinners. The theme of redemption does not, however, eclipse the themes of creation and sovereign rulership. Indeed, our redeemer, Jesus Christ the Lord, is revealed to be the One through whom the Father sustains the universe (see John 1, Colossians 1 and Hebrews 1). 'He is before all things, and in him all things hold together' (Colossians 1:17; see also Hebrews 1:2–3).

The fact that the triune God created all things and continues to sustain them is foundational in Scripture. He is no absentee landlord, who set the universe in operation and then left it to run on its own. He is the God of today in whom 'we live and move and have our being' (Acts 17:28).

We are not left to fend for ourselves in some merciless corner of cold space. The saints of the ages call to us:

Come, let us sing for joy to the LORD;
    let us shout aloud to the Rock of our salvation.
Let us come before him with thanksgiving
    and extol him with music and song.
For the LORD is the great God,
    the great King above all gods.
In his hand are the depths of the earth,
    and the mountain peaks belong to him.
The sea is his, for he made it,
    and his hands formed the dry land.
Come, let us bow down in worship,
    let us kneel before the LORD our Maker;
for he is our God
    and we are the people of his pasture,
the flock under his care
(Psalm 95:1–7).

Wonderful truth! God, the infinite Creator of all things, has chosen to cherish us as a shepherd cherishes his flock.

There is a profound difference here, however. Sheep see their shepherd, but no man has ever seen God. Sheep hear the call of the shepherd; people very, very rarely hear the actual voice of God. Because of the silent, invisible nature of God, we may quickly lose perspective and drift through life as if God doesn't exist. Fortunately, God left behind a silent witness to his majesty: the very creation itself. But we must look. We must listen.

'The heavens declare the glory of God; the skies proclaim the work of his hands. Day after day they pour forth speech; night after night they display knowledge' (Psalm 19:1–2). To sensitive souls, everything joins in a thunderous silence proclaiming the wonders of God.

As we would expect, Jesus was sensitive to the message of creation; this led him to give his disciples lessons about salt and light, the rising of the sun and the falling of the rain. He pointed out the need to store treasure in heaven rather than hoard treasures on earth, where 'moth and rust destroy'. He drew lessons from the birds of the air and the flowers of the field (Matthew 5:13,45; 6:19,26,28).

The scriptural injunction is clear: we can only maintain perspective if we go through life recognizing that

This is my Father's world, and to my listening ears
All nature sings, and round me rings the music of the spheres.
This is my Father's world: I rest me in the thought
Of rocks and trees, of skies and seas—his hand the wonders wrought.[1]

This isn't easy. We spend most of our lives inside climate-controlled buildings. Without care, we quickly lose perspective, forget God's presence and live as if everything depended on us. Through the help of the Spirit, we need to cultivate the habit of recognizing God's fingerprints wherever we look in creation so that we can lift our hearts in spontaneous worship and thanksgiving.

If we live in cities and have little exposure to the countryside, we can still see God's infinite skill in the fingers that we use to play over computer keyboards, the smiles of our children and the sunshine that streams in through the windows.

Let me confess at the beginning of this book that I have as much difficulty as you in maintaining perspective. I have to keep reminding myself to recognize God's handiwork in the world around me. The devotions that follow incorporate the lessons I've drawn for my own life from the scenes along our country road. I share them with the prayer that they will become a blessing to you.

Prayer

Blessed Lord, open my eyes to recognize all the evidences of your creative majesty along our country road—and beyond. Help me to see your hand in the passing seasons, in the creatures of the forest, in the plants along the stream, in the sky above and in the earth beneath. Help me to live from day to day and to serve others without forgetting to worship you. Help me to draw strength and comfort not only from the Scriptures, but also from the evidences of your wisdom and power spread out all around me. What an awesome God you are! The whole earth is full of your glory. Artist! Engineer! Sculptor! Playwright! Father! Redeemer! Friend! Amen.

Notes

1 Maltbie D. Babcock.

january

Broken tree

Bible reading
Psalm 139, especially verses 23–24

A ll night the wind howled. The house groaned in protest. In the morning, I wandered around our property to survey the damage. Broken branches littered the ground. To the north, the gale had felled a woodpecker-riddled tree. To the south, I discovered that the wind had snapped off the top half of one of our Scotch pines. Not just any Scotch pine, but the climbing tree favoured by one of our granddaughters—the tree with the regular whorls of branches. The crown lay ten feet away in a grove of broken sumachs. Upon closer inspection, I discovered that the wind had broken it off just at the point where a canker had weakened the tree.

As with the weakened tree, it's easy to overlook flaws in our characters that render us susceptible to disaster during times of great temptation. They hide below the surface of our respectability until exposed by extreme stress. In Psalms 19 and 139, David describes how he learned about this personality peril the hard way. Bitter experience taught him the danger of overlooking his own sins. The memory of Nathan's accusation, 'Thou art the man', rang in his memory.

In Psalm 139, David urged the Lord, 'Search me, O God, and know my heart; test me and know my anxious thoughts. See if there is any offensive way in me, and lead me in the way everlasting' (vv. 22-23). Failure to recognize our own sinful attitudes doesn't mean that they aren't present. David wrote, 'Who can discern his errors? Forgive my hidden faults. Keep your servant also from wilful sins; may they not rule over me' (Psalm 19:12–13).

Keeping our lives open to God in prayer is the only way to discover the inherent folly within us. Jeremiah wrote a great truth that Christians often use in challenging sinners to come to Christ. 'The heart is deceitful above all things and beyond cure. Who can understand it? I the LORD search the heart and examine the mind' (Jeremiah 17:9–10). This verse speaks to us all, warning us how easy it is to be self-deceived. This twisted propensity makes it imperative that we daily submit ourselves to the convicting work of the Holy Spirit. Danger may lie camouflaged beneath the surface of our professions of faith. We seldom recognize the self-sins: self-love, self-serving, self-doubt. Why? They often hide beneath a cloak of self-confidence.

If we discipline ourselves to read the Scriptures devotionally—not legalistically—the Spirit can use the Word to uncover hidden faults. We should view each day's meditation as an opportunity for God to cast light into the darkest recesses of our hearts. Consider, for example, praying through the Beatitudes. 'Lord, am I humble [poor in spirit]? Do I feel remorse for my sins [mourn]? Am I aggressive, competitive or meek? Do I long more for rich foods or consumer goods than I do for righteousness?'

We can ask the Spirit to probe our hearts as we read about the failings of Bible characters, study the Gospels or meditate on the epistles. A complete openness to passages such as Ephesians 4:32 can have a profound cleansing effect: 'Be kind and compassionate to one another, forgiving each other, just as in Christ God forgave you.' Unforgiveness often lies deeply buried beneath years of memories.

Like the unseen canker in my pine tree, hidden weaknesses of character, and even secret sins, reside in all of us. Experience taught David to flee to the throne of grace for light to be cast on his unrecognized sins. Exposure led to deliverance from their danger.

The more we understand the infinite love of God displayed in Christ, the less we will need to pretend to be what we are not. Consider Jesus' tender words to Peter before his denial: 'Simon, Simon, Satan has asked to sift you as wheat. But I have prayed for you, Simon, that your faith may not fail' (Luke 22:31–32). Satan desires to destroy us through exploiting our hidden flaws. But Christ will pray for us that our faith fail not—even when temptation blows like a hurricane through our lives.

Prayer
Lord Jesus, continue to pray for me that my faith may not fail. Use the Word gently to expose my flaws and sinful attitudes. Keep my heart open to your convicting presence. But deliver me

from despair or depression when my fallen nature lies exposed. Instead, assure me of your love, forgiveness and presence. Deliver me from temptations that might overwhelm me. Lead me on, higher and higher, I pray. Amen.

Partridge in a pear tree

Bible reading
Matthew 6:25–34

Early one winter morning, I dimly perceived some dark shapes in one of our wild cherry trees. Looking closer, I realized that they were ruffled grouse. I counted six of them nibbling on the tender buds at the ends of the smallest branches. Foot-deep snow had made it impossible for them to find forage on the forest floor. Clearly, the Creator had a back-up plan to care for them in emergencies. They returned every day at dawn and in the evening, until the spring thaw finally banished the snow.

A day or two after I first saw them, I made the connection. Remember that non-Christmas carol, *The Twelve Days of Christmas*? Each stanza ends with 'And a partridge in a pear tree'. I've always thought it a silly song. After all, what business have partridges in pear trees? My opinion of the song hasn't changed much, but now I can see a glimmer of truth shining through the lyrics.

Pear trees and cherry trees are in the same genus (family). Partridges and grouse also share biological similarities. Could it be that, centuries ago, the song-writer noticed partridges nibbling twigs in pear trees near where he lived in England?

God provides for partridges—and for his children. 'Look at the birds of the air; they do not sow or reap or store away in barns, and yet your heavenly Father feeds them. Are you not much more valuable than they?' (Matthew 6:26). I think God must have sent the grouse to my woodlot to remind me of his providential care—like the time back in Bible college when I was broke but knew I should travel home at Christmas to be with my largely non-Christian family. Hitch-hiking north from South Carolina, one ride took me way off course. But the next ride had been specially arranged by God to impress this struggling disciple. The man who picked me up took me home and, after calling up his insurance agent, handed me the keys to his Corvette sports car. I could hardly contain my excitement as I drove north to Buffalo. From the money he gave me for gas, I had enough left over to take the bus to Toronto! Oh, and the man who *happened* to sit down by me in the bus station that evening gave me a bed overnight and fed me breakfast in the morning. He didn't *look* like an angel, but ...

During our first term as missionaries in Pakistan, our money completely ran out. Just in time, money from a mysterious legacy arrived. We learned that my father, an airman, had stayed with a family in a private home in Britain during the First World War. The family had kept in touch with my father through the years. Discovering that one of his sons was a missionary, the woman of the house included me in her will. Who but God could engineer the arrival of money years later, in a foreign country, at a time when we were totally broke!

As missionaries, when our needs were the greatest, God frequently gave us dramatic evidences of his providential care. Who would think that he would use my father, who considered my missionary calling to be a waste of education and talent?

My father was a builder who owned several houses. For tax purposes, he transferred the family home into my mother's name. Unknown to us, my mother—the only Christian in my family—arranged in her will for us to receive the family home after the passing of my father. When my father died, we were stunned to receive word of this behest. What a marvellous provision!

By provisions large and small, God cares for us: the helpmates he chooses for us; the careers he steers us into; the friends he brings into our lives; the events that upset our plans; ah, yes, even the troubles that challenge our faith; and, hardest of all, the illnesses that threaten our very lives.

When an angiogram revealed the blockage of key arteries in my heart, I realized my dreams of long hikes and canoe trips would have to be shelved. Evidently, I was not a candidate for heart bypass surgery. Pills would become my portion. What a shocking and totally unexpected confrontation with mortality!

Could this be providence? How, Lord? 'Well,' he seemed to whisper, 'you've got a lot to learn. First, you've never been very empathetic with those who are ill. Second, well ... one thing at a time.' Several years later, I must admit that the benefits are manifold. I have more empathy for others.

I eat a healthier diet. I walk more regularly. And most days I can say, 'Thank you, Lord, for another day of grace.' But I haven't yet reached the pinnacle represented by the young mother in our Bible study, who said recently, 'I praise God for having had cancer.' God's way of providing for us is very mysterious.

Prayer
Thank you, Lord, for a lesson from the birds. Thank you for your providential care. And among your provisions are a host of gifts much more important than Corvettes and houses. Help me to recognize the value of these other gifts. Amen.

The winter blues

Bible reading
Proverbs 4:1–19

For weeks, cloud cover obscured the sun. Some days, there was intermittent light snow. Throughout this season, short, very cold days alternated with days of thaw, creating slush everywhere. People were crabby, short-tempered. Scowls adorned otherwise cheerful faces. Many of us found ourselves gripped by the winter blues.

Like the birds that migrate south, winter-weary citizens feel the pull of warmer climes. Some snowbirds fly to Florida, Arizona, the Caribbean or Spain. If, perchance, our bank accounts can bear it, we may even wing our way to Bali, Fiji or Australia. Who can deny the delight of sauntering down a sandy beach under a tropical sun, while our compatriots back home shiver in the cold or slog through slush on their way to work?

Unfortunately, many of us cannot afford a sun-drenched holiday. May I suggest another option? That we turn our faces towards celestial light: 'the LORD God is a sun and shield' (Psalm 84:11). We can rise from sleep before the watery winter sun appears, open our Bibles and soak our souls with the light that streams from the Scriptures. We can meditate on the excellencies of God. 'God is a spirit, infinite, eternal and unchangeable in his being, wisdom, power, holiness, justice, goodness and truth.'[1] As we give thought to each of his attributes, God's spiritual light infuses our souls. Our burdens are lifted. Our spirits soar aloft on the wings of worship. A day begun in worship is less likely to end in melancholy.

But can meditation really change our moods? Jesus teaches us in the Beatitudes that the attitudes we bring to life affect every arena of human enterprise. I've often noticed how the attitude a saint brings to his or her circumstances transforms that saint's whole approach: relationships, work environment and, especially, moods. In Proverbs we read, 'The path of the righteous is like the first gleam of dawn, shining ever brighter till the full light of day' (Proverbs 4:18). Need winter stifle that progress? Not if 'Your word is a lamp to my feet and a light for my path' (Psalm 119:105). Add to that the promise of Christ: 'I am the light of the world. Whoever follows me will never walk in darkness, but will have the light of life' (John 8:12).

Impractical, you say. Yes, it sounds impractical—even insensitive to those who suffer most. And those of us who find the winter less taxing should offer understanding and companionship to those who deal with very real depression during this time of the year. Some sufferers may need medical intervention.

May all of us, however, embrace the call of Christ to overcome moods too dependent on our external environment. Being overcomers involves not just victory on the spiritual battlefield but also triumph in the arena of challenging circumstances. I find it helpful to view the winter months positively, as a welcome opportunity to inject new life into those goals that have become anaemic; to complete tasks interrupted by the lure of spring wildflowers or summer jaunts. Since I'm a writer, winter is the season to finish the manuscript I've been delaying. It's time to catch up on those magazines that have piled up, read those important books I've set aside, hone my writing craft, complete that woodworking project, visit the colleague I haven't seen in years.

You may want to sign up for that course you've always wanted to take. Or embrace that hobby you've dreamed about. Or begin that exercise programme you know is needed. Take a friend out to dinner. Write a letter of encouragement. Winter gives us time to do things, and time is infinitely precious!

Prayer

Lord, help me to be led by the light that streams from the reigning Christ, and not be rendered melancholy by a grey winter day. Enable me to be purposeful, energized, focused and constructive. Help me to grow in grace, whether sunshine sparkles off the snow or the sun hides its face. Remind me that you are the light of the world and that whoever believes in you will not abide in darkness [John 12:46]. Amen.

Notes

1 *Westminster Shorter Catechism*, Q. 4: What is God?

Guilt and winter holidays

Bible reading
1 Timothy 4:1–8

Winter is the time to take a holiday in some sunny clime, far from ice and snow. Or is it? We deserve a break from short, cold days—don't we? Those of us with tender consciences may raise questions. What about the cost? Couldn't the money be better used to help AIDS orphans in Africa—or at least to reduce a home mortgage? And what about the time involved? Couldn't it be better spent in helping Habitat For Humanity build houses or taking a theological course, or spending a week volunteering for evangelism? Is this a guilty conscience speaking? Or is it the devil confusing us in order to spoil our enjoyment of life?

Questions such as these highlight the need to distinguish between genuine and false guilt. In mankind's original state of purity and innocence, the conscience could be trusted to warn of evil and commend right actions. Adam and Eve felt genuinely guilty when they disobeyed God's command in the Garden. In the aftermath of their fall into sin, however, the human conscience, along with everything else, became corrupted. As a result, it cannot be treated as infallible. The conscience can be evil (Hebrews 10:22) or good (1 Timothy 1:5); weak (1 Corinthians 8:7) or clear (1 Timothy 3:9; 1 Peter 3:16); defiled (Titus 1:15), seared (1 Timothy 4:2) or dead (Ephesians 4:17–19).

Everyone is born with the basic principles of God's universal law written on the heart—everyone has a conscience: 'since they show that the requirements of the law are written on their hearts, their consciences also bearing witness, and their thought now accusing, now even defending them' (Romans 2:15).

The conscience does not stay pure long. Traditions, upbringing and false teaching, in so far as they are contrary to God's law, distort and erode the dependability of the conscience. At the time of our conversions, our consciences may be defiled, weak, seared or even dead. Then we hear the gospel. The Holy Spirit convicts us of breaking God's laws. We feel guilt, repent and respond to the gospel of Christ. We are saved! We feel great relief in knowing that our sins are forgiven. But the work of sanctification is only just beginning.

The Holy Spirit takes on the task of retraining the consciences of new believers so that they react accurately to God's will. The author of Hebrews encourages us to embrace the influence of the Spirit: 'let us draw near to God with a sincere heart in full assurance of faith, having our hearts sprinkled to cleanse us from a guilty conscience' (Hebrews 10:22). Those who can approach God freely and confidently show the presence of a sincere heart—a cleansed conscience—untroubled by false guilt. Echoing a similar theme, Paul highlights love as the main focus of the renewed conscience, because love is the fulfilment of the law: 'The goal of this command is love, which comes from a pure heart and a good conscience and a sincere faith' (1 Timothy 1:5).

Delivering believers from false guilt is not easy. Paul warned Timothy about false teachers who distort the gospel and use guilt to manipulate their disciples: 'They forbid people to marry and order them to abstain from certain foods, which God created to be received with thanksgiving by those who believe and who know the truth. For everything God created is good, and nothing is to be rejected if it is received with thanksgiving' (1 Timothy 4:3–4). Clearly, believers are expected to enjoy God's gifts with a clear conscience, gifts that include sex in marriage and good food at the dinner table.

A host of other issues troubles many Christians. How should I dress when I go to church—suit and tie? Am I bound to attend every meeting my church schedules? Should I have personal devotions in the morning or the evening? What if I miss a day? How much TV should I watch? Is it permissible for a Christian to read fiction? (See Paul's treatment of questionable practices in Romans 14 and 15.)

Having a biblically sensitive conscience untroubled by legalistic guilt is the Christian ideal. So, should we feel guilty about taking a winter holiday? Probably not. The Old Testament Sabbath and festival principles make generous provision for rest from work. Should we use a reasonable amount of money on ourselves, after giving generously to God's works? Probably we should.

Answering practical questions such as these is not easy, and answers will vary according to the individual. As we struggle to find answers, we need to remember that God desires our joy, while Satan promotes misery, uncertainty and false guilt. If the devil can't tempt us to sin outright, he is determined to make us miserable even when we seek to serve God.

Prayer

Heavenly Father, I am so thankful that you are a good God: generous, loving and merciful. Thank you for all your good gifts. But sometimes, Lord, I feel guilty about what I have and how I use my time. Send your Spirit to sort through any confusion I have and to bring clear conviction where I am straying from your will. And may he fill my heart with the joy and peace that is my heritage in Christ. Where confusion and false guilt are being used by Satan to rob me of my heritage in Christ, deliver me from his wiles. In Jesus' name. Amen.

february

The neatness wars

Bible reading
1 Corinthians 13

Can marriage survive the neatness wars? Mary Helen feels called to organize household space so that it is open, understated and immaculate. In my office, piles of magazines and papers suit me fine. They might come in handy for my research some day. And I need pens, paper clips, sticky notes, yellow markers and coffee cups near at hand. I'm insecure unless I can plaster several bulletin boards with notes on things I might get to. I believe space is to be used—fully.

The day after 'the garlic affair', I thought I had ammunition to curb Mary Helen's passion to tidy up. One day, while making everything shipshape, Mary Helen arrived at the laundry room, where I lay out garlic and sundry other items to dry. Most of the useable garlic had already flavoured curries and soups. A few wizened bulbs of garlic remained— which she trashed. Then she turned her attention to a dish full of much firmer bulbs. Slicing them up, she dumped them into the pot for supper.

That night when we sat down to enjoy our stew, I noticed these pale bits scattered through the dish. I made no comment on their rather bland flavour. The next day, however, when I went into the laundry room, I noticed that my gladioli bulbs were missing. After inquiry, I discovered that, yes, Mary Helen had mistaken the gladioli bulbs for garlic! Through hoots of laughter, I dimly perceived a weapon to use in my attempts to curb her penchant for neatness.

Not that I can use this tale much: she denies it ever happened! Fortunately, I don't need to use it as leverage. Years of good-natured sparring have mellowed us to the point where we give each other a lot of leeway. Experience has taught us that the very differences that attracted us to each other can easily spark disagreements. Rather than argue, it's much better to agree on a compromise. Mary Helen lets me do just what I want in my office—as long as I vacuum regularly and dust occasionally. I give her free reign in the kitchen, the dining room and even the bedroom. She grants me freedom in the garage.

The Bible has a lot of great advice for getting along with others: 'Accept one another, then, just as Christ accepted you' (Romans 15:7); 'Be completely humble and gentle; be patient, bearing with one another in love' (Ephesians 4:2). If I try to curb Mary Helen's fondness for a tidy house, we'll both end up unhappy; better to accept her and celebrate her marvellous personality. What a boring marriage it would be if we were the same! I must admit, I'm rather proud of what she's done in the living room. And she does come to me when she needs something from one of my files or to fix a broken appliance.

Every relationship, not just the marital union, requires a lot of give and take and tons of humour. In business, in the family, among our neighbours, with our relatives—and certainly on the national and international scene— learning to be forbearing is more valuable than learning how to win arguments. 'Love is patient … it is not self-seeking, it is not easily angered, it keeps no record of wrongs' (1 Corinthians 13:4–5). Love, which includes forbearance, is the oil that keeps relationships from squeaking and squealing worse than the hinges on a rusty garden gate.

Of course, no relationship is perfect. In spite of our negotiated treaty on spheres of influence, Mary Helen will occasionally frown and say, 'Honey, can you tidy up the garage? The kids are coming for the weekend and it's really looking messy.'

She's probably right, but if my defences are down, I may respond, 'Hey, I'm organized. I know exactly where everything is! Just relax. Your problem is that you're compulsive.'

Those are fighting words, best left unsaid. Time to say, 'I'm sorry,' and make up. 'Bear with each other and forgive whatever grievances you may have against one another. Forgive as the Lord forgave you' (Colossians 3:13).

Prayer

Heavenly Father, we're all so different. Husbands and wives; neighbours; colleagues; relatives: we have different likes and dislikes. We like different colours and foods and clothing. We vote for different people. Help me to accept those differences—even when they seem so strange. Enable me to be a patient, loving and encouraging person, who is quick to overlook personal quirks and foibles. After all, you have accepted me through Jesus Christ. Amen.

Distinctive trees—
diverse people

Bible reading
Romans 12:1–8

I was astounded at one man's response when invited to hike in the woods: 'No, thanks. If you've seen one tree, you've seen them all.' Nothing could be further from the truth!

Every tree is distinctive. Evergreens keep their needles all year, while deciduous trees drop their leaves in the fall. Some pines have needles in clusters of five and some in clusters of two; some have needles that spiral, while others appear long or feathery. Even without their leaves, trees can be identified by their overall shape, the texture of their bark or the look of their twigs. Twig structures vary widely: some twigs are fat, some skinny, some pointed, some blunt and some hairy.

Trees also vary in cellular structure. Cut any tree into lumber and the differences become apparent. Oak flooring differs greatly from flooring cut from sugar maple, beech or birch. Some wood is dense and hard; other wood is soft and malleable.

Like diverse species of trees, individuals in the church receive from the Spirit different gifts. Healthy churches thrive where diverse gifts are exercised. Imagine if one church had a glut of teachers but none had gifts of mercy, giving or helpfulness! Like a forest composed of only one or two species, a church in which members exercise just a few gifts is a church in danger. Fire or insect infestation quickly destroys a forest with only one or two species of trees.

Fortunately, like our northern hardwood forests, the Holy Spirit fills our churches with people who have differing gifts. Four passages in the New Testament deal extensively with spiritual gifts: Romans 12:3–8; 1 Corinthians 12:1–11,27–31; Ephesians 4:7–13; 1 Peter 4:8–11. These passages teach that every believer has one or more gifts and that these gifts are 'given for the common good' (1 Corinthians 12:7). 'Each one should use whatever gift he has received to serve others, faithfully administering God's grace in its various forms' (1 Peter 4:10). The gifts are given 'so that the body of Christ may be built up' (Ephesians 4:12).

Spiritual gifts are not identical with natural talents or abilities but are special enablements of the Holy Spirit. He takes our varied training, abilities and talents and focuses these endowments in a particular ministry direction. This ministry focus is our spiritual gift. For many, the gift remains latent, a potentiality to serve that awaits opportunity or development.

Spiritual gifts are not something we choose like gifts under a Christmas tree. They are gifts of grace, undeserved and unearned. From my study of the texts, I have concluded that there are around fifteen spiritual gifts whose exercise is crucial to the healthy growth and operation of a church.

Consider those mentioned in Romans 12 (for a fuller treatment, see my book *Church: No Spectator Sport*[1]):
- *Prophecy*—forth-telling or preaching.
- *Serving*—helping practically.
- *Teaching*—communicating biblical truth with an aim to change behaviour.
- *Encouragement*—uplifting and inspiring others.
- *Giving*—using resources to supply kingdom finances.
- *Administration or leadership*—envisioning what should be, formulating a plan and inspiring others to participate in the extension of the kingdom.
- *Mercy*— empathizing practically with those in misery or distress.

Other passages mention further gifts:
- *Apostleship*—a gift given only to the apostles, but partially carried on through the pioneer church-planting ministry of missionaries.
- *Evangelism*—an ability to lead the unsaved to faith in Christ.
- *Knowledge*—an ability to research and systematize biblical content.
- *Wisdom*—a capability to apply scriptural knowledge to concrete situations.
- *Hospitality*—an ability to use one's home to serve and encourage others.

- *Faith*—an unshakable faith in God in the face of insurmountable obstacles.
- *Discernment*—an ability to distinguish between truth and error, good and evil, and between genuine and hypocritical expressions of the Christian faith.

Sincere Christians have differing views on the exact nature of some gifts, particularly those of apostleship, prophecy, knowledge, tongues, interpretation, miracles and healing. Instead of plunging into controversy, wisdom would lead us to embrace wholeheartedly the gifts that are clearly defined. For example, without the exercise of the gifts of teaching, evangelism, encouragement and mercy, the house of God cannot be built as God designed it.

A variety of building materials—spruce, pine, oak and concrete—go into the construction of most houses. A house built only of concrete is cold and uninviting. Similarly, a church where a variety of gifted people do not participate becomes cold and uninteresting. The church is meant to radiate the warmth and charm that come from a congregation of happily involved believers who use their gifts to serve one another and their community.

Prayer

Lord Jesus, I praise you for the way you designed your body, the church, so that everyone has a task and the spiritual gifts to fulfil that task. Enable me to pitch in with energy, using my gifts to edify the church. And, Lord Jesus, where there seems to be a lack of giftedness in my congregation, fan latent gifts into usefulness. Help each person in my congregation to feel special and needed. Amen.

Notes

1 **Eric E. Wright,** *Church: No Spectator Sport* (Darlington: Evangelical Press, 1994).

Do disasters herald judgement?

Bible reading
Amos 4

Whenever we turn on the TV, we see reports of disasters of one kind or another. Recently, unprecedented snowfalls blanketed the west coast, knocking out power for days. Ice storms have had the same effect in the US Midwest. Meanwhile, wildfires rage in California and mudslides bury villages in the Philippines.

Are disasters a wake-up call from God? Are they harbingers of judgement to come? Drought; famine; hurricanes; earthquakes; tsunamis; devastating diseases, such as AIDS; the carnage in Iraq; terrorism: are happenings such as these just the coincidental clash of natural or human forces?

Certainly, Christ warned us to watch out for signs of his return and the judgement to come: 'You will hear of wars and rumours of wars ... Nation will rise against nation, and kingdom against kingdom. There will be famines and earthquakes in various places' (Matthew 24:6–7). These are 'the beginning of birth pains' (v. 8). They will precede a time of 'great distress, unequalled from the beginning of the world until now' (v. 21).

It is fair to assume that disastrous events, along with 'the increase of wickedness' that we see all around us, are meant to remind us to 'Keep watch, because you do not know on what day your Lord will come' (Matthew 24:42). The biblical record of the flood in Noah's day warns us to be watchful and faithful lest the day of Christ's return find us unprepared.

The Old Testament prophets were in no doubt about the purpose of disasters. Consider, for example, the words of Amos. Worship in Israel had become hypocritical and ritualistic. The people bragged about their piety (see Amos 4:1–5). But God condemned them for injustice ('They trample on the heads of the poor'—2:7), immorality ('Father and son use the same girl'—2:7) and drunken idolatry ('They lie down beside every altar … In the house of their god they drink wine'—2:8). The hearts of Israel—and Judah—were far from the Lord. God responded, 'I hate, I despise your religious feasts … But let justice roll on like a river, righteousness like a never-failing stream' (5:21,24).

Sadly, Israel ignored all God's warnings. He had sent drought and famine, blight and mildew to no avail. There had been lack of rain in some areas and abundance of rain in others. A locust plague devastated their fig and olive trees. They lost many young men in wars (see 4:6–11). After the description of each disaster, Amos records a refrain: '"yet you have not returned to me," declares the LORD' (4:6,8–11). Israel's failure to repent provoked God to declare, ' … prepare to meet your God, O Israel' (4:12).

Inevitably, judgement fell. In 722 BC, Assyria besieged Samaria and conquered the northern kingdom of Israel. In 586 BC, Babylon conquered the southern kingdom of Judah, destroying Jerusalem and its temple. Still God's people did not learn. Once again, in AD 70, Jerusalem and its temple were destroyed, this time by the Romans.

In Amos 3 we read a difficult truth that explains much about God's dealings with his people: 'When disaster comes to a city, has not the Lord caused it? Surely the Sovereign Lord does nothing without revealing his plan to his servants the prophets' (vv. 6–7). As reflected by this verse, the Old Testament is full of prophetic warnings delivered during times of disaster. Can we interpret this to mean that all disasters are warnings from God? In the case of Old Testament Israel, this seems to be the case. But Israel was a theocracy, with God as its sovereign King. No nation today has this status. Nevertheless, the prophetic portions of the New Testament—and the teaching of Christ in particular—do give us some basis to apply this truth to our situations.

Paul declared that the things that happened to Israel 'occurred as examples to keep us from setting our hearts on evil things as they did' (1 Corinthians 10:6). And yet, in spite of biblical warnings, today's societies are as corrupt as ever: materialistic; violent; dishonest. Immorality has become so common that most people assume that sex before marriage is the norm, sex with multiple partners is OK, homosexuality is normal, abortion is a right and divorce should be easy. Drunkenness and drugs; child abuse: the degradation of Western society seems to be rising to a zenith. And, by and large, people are complacent.

Can judgement be far off? In spite of the testimony of both history and the Scriptures, do we think that our own nations will escape the judgement of God? 'Woe to you who are complacent in Zion, and to you who feel secure on Mount Samaria' (Amos 6:1). Whether or not modern disasters foretell the coming of judgement, we would be wise to face our sins squarely and repent. Our nations desperately need to recognize their danger. 'Seek the LORD while he may be found; call on him while he is near. Let the wicked forsake his way and the evil man his thoughts. Let him turn to the LORD, and he will have mercy on him, and to our God, for he will freely pardon' (Isaiah 55:6–7).

Prayer
Almighty God, awaken our nation to its danger. Call the complacent to repentance. May every TV picture of a disaster warn us of coming judgement. Send revival. Begin in my heart today. Amen.

When plans don't work out

Bible reading
James 4:13–17

The week had been full of appointments and preparation for an important quarterly editorial meeting. The night before the meeting, I breathed a sigh of relief. The agenda was printed. The papers copied. For once, I was ready.

Then one of the committee members called to direct my attention to the weather report. The next day promised to dawn with sixty-mile-per-hour winds, plunging temperatures and the possibility of heavy snow. I had been so focused on planning and preparation, I hadn't listened to the weather report. The caller suggested that it might be best to cancel the meeting in light of the distance people had to travel. I was reluctant because rescheduling is always difficult. But I agreed.

I like to plan things—to organize. I echo the TV character who used to chortle, 'I just love it when a plan comes together.' Fortunately, circumstances often force changes in my plans. Fortunately? Yes, because God's plan is always better than my plan.

The uncertainty generated by broken plans reminds us to stop counting on tomorrow and to start trusting God: 'do not worry about your life ... If ... God clothes the grass of the field, which is here today and tomorrow is thrown into the fire, will he not much more clothe you, O you of little faith? So do not worry ... seek first his kingdom and his righteousness ... do not worry about tomorrow, for tomorrow will worry about itself' (Matthew 6:25,30–31,33–34). People who trust God for tomorrow escape a lot of stress and worry.

James cautions us about getting our hearts set on something that may or may not work out. In every situation we need to say, 'If it is the Lord's will, we will live and do this or that' (James 4:15). When we follow James' advice and consciously submit ourselves to the Lord's will, we save ourselves enormous frustration. Flexibility begins to characterize our lives. We're able to adjust to changing circumstances without the cynicism of William Henley, who wrote,

Out of the night that covers me,
Black as the Pit from pole to pole,
I thank whatever gods may be
For my unconquerable soul.

In the fell clutch of circumstance,
I have not winced nor cried aloud;
Under the bludgeonings of chance
My head is bloody, but unbowed ...

I am the master of my fate;
I am the captain of my soul.[1]

What a sad poem! Unlike Henley, if dark circumstances derail our plans, we can reach out by faith and touch the true Captain of our souls. We can let him lead us through the darkness. As his children, we know that, though the present may seem dark and our plans lie broken at our feet like shards of glass, God's will is 'good, pleasing and perfect' (Romans 12:2). Some day, the light will shine and understanding will dawn. In the meantime, he calls us to walk by faith in his sovereign providence.

Prayer

Heavenly Father, I know you don't want me to stop planning. But help me to build flexibility into my plans and stop expecting everything I want to happen. Enable me to accept your will, even when it runs contrary to my dearest desires or most thoroughly researched plans. Lord Jesus, you promised to be with me for ever. Take my hand and lead me on into the future with the confidence that comes from trust in you. Amen.

Notes

1 **William Ernest Henley,** 'Echoes', No. 4, stanzas 1,2,4, in **John Bartlett,** *Bartlett's Familiar Quotations* (Boston & Toronto: Little, Brown & Co., 1980), p. 663.

march

Is there a human homing instinct?

Bible reading
Acts 17:16–34

Giant rainbow trout have been leaving the deep places in Lake Ontario to search out the mouth of the Ganaraska River. Attracted by the lure of these outsized fish, fishermen gather from miles around to line the banks. Serious and silent, bundled up against the chill, they angle for one of the fabled trout whose unerring instinct leads them to fight their way up the river to spawn.

A grand variety of birds, also led by instinct, arrive from sunny climes far to the south. Among the earliest are the robins, who quickly activate their worm radar and search our greening lawn for fat worms. The killdeer soar and sing above the fields. Red-winged blackbirds scout the marshes for likely nesting sites. Mourning doves hover and coo. Geese and ducks throng the Garden Hill pond and scavenge in the stubble of valley cornfields.

A-a-a-h, it's that time of year again. Lord, how wonderful you are! ' ... you renew the face of the earth' (Psalm 104:30). You send your winged heralds to introduce the arrival of this delightful season. I stand in awe of the instinct you created in birds that moves them to leave the warmth and bounty of the south to wing their flight north even before the snow melts.

While mammals, birds and fish return to their places each year, we often fail to return to the God who created us. Yet there is something unquenchably religious programmed into human DNA.

Atheists deny any inherent instinct to acknowledge, even seek, God. In their view, belief in the supernatural is a primitive evolutionary response to fears of the unknown. Atheists hope that, as science expands our understanding of the universe, religion will die away. They remain disappointed.

Likewise, anthropologists committed to the evolutionary hypothesis find some discoveries inconvenient—deserving of suppression. In their view, religion evolved from primitive animism into idolatry and, finally, into its highest form, monotheism.

But in point of fact, '90 percent of the world's folk religions are permeated with monotheistic presuppositions' much more ancient than their current practices.[1] The Inca, for example, had an almost extinct memory of *Virachocha*—the Lord, the omnipotent Creator of all things.

The more recent practices of the Santal of India—to appease spirits, carry out sorcery and worship the sun—developed after their original worship of the Good God, *Thakur Jiu*, faded from their memory. An elder explained to the Norwegian missionary Skrefsrud that, in the beginning, the Santal had obeyed only *Thakur*.

'Dr. Wilhelm Schmidt, an Austrian, set out in the 1920s to compile every "alias of the Almighty" which researchers had discovered around the world … It took six volumes totaling 4,500 pages to detail them all! And at least a thousand more examples have come to light since then.'[2] Unfortunately, while the National Geographic Society bombards us with tales of evolution—and very beautiful videos—research such as Schmidt's has been consigned to oblivion.

The student of the Scriptures, of course, is not surprised with Schmidt's findings. Believers know that God created people in his own image with a heart that is restless until it finds rest in him. How could God's image-bearers be content with material things when 'He has also set eternity in the hearts of men' (Ecclesiastes 3:11)?

In Athens, Paul brought to the attention of idolatrous Greeks an altar in their midst dedicated to 'An Unknown God'. He proceeded to explain that this mysterious God is 'The God who made the world and everything in it … [who] made every nation of men, that they should inhabit the whole earth … so that men would seek him and perhaps reach out for him and find him, though he is not far from each one of us' (Acts 17:24,26–27).

Paul went on to quote their own writers: '"For in him we live and move and have our being." As some of your own poets have said, "We are his offspring"' (v. 28).

A hunger for God? A thirst for intimacy with the Most High? A God-seeking gene?

The prophet Isaiah sends out an invitation: 'Come, all you who are thirsty ... Why ... labour on what does not satisfy? ... Seek the LORD while he may be found; call on him while he is near' (Isaiah 55:1–2,6). Jesus understood the impossibility of human yearning being satisfied outside of God. This led him to appeal to his hearers in a special way. Among other things, he offered them living water, the bread of life, the light of the world, peace with God and, over all, his love (see John 4,6,8,14,16). Perhaps there is indeed a human gene that makes us restless until we find satisfaction in God.

Prayer

Lord, deliver me from seeking ultimate satisfaction in food or acquisitions, work or hobbies, reading or travel, sports or sex. Like the hummingbirds who return each spring to our feeder, may I return each day to you for spiritual sustenance, encouragement and inspiration. And, Lord, arouse within people everywhere a yearning to find you, the one true God. Grant our missionaries success in satisfying that yearning. Amen.

Notes

1 **Don Richardson,** *Eternity in their Hearts* (Ventura, CA: Regal Books, 1981), p. 44.
2 Ibid.

A time to gather stones

Bible reading
1 Timothy 6:6–19

Some of the Preacher's teachings in Ecclesiastes are very hard to fathom. Take, for example, what he says in chapter 3: 'There is a time for everything, and a season for every activity under heaven' (v. 1). I appreciate the need for a season of planting, but uprooting? Of gathering stones and scattering stones?

Understanding dawned the year we moved to our first country home. The rolling hills of Northumberland reflect the inexorable crush of the ice age and its aftermath. All across Ontario we find the signs of the great melt that ended this mysterious period: vast areas of alluvial gravel and sand; strange hills and ridges (called drumlins and eskers); deep gouges and scratches in the granite of the Canadian Shield from rocks frozen into the ice sheet; stones of all sizes randomly dropped over the landscape.

In this part of the world, spring thaw is a season for gathering up the stones that winter's frost has brought to the surface. In pioneer days, as soon as the ground dried, farmers hitched their stone boats behind a horse or mule and circled the fields collecting the spring harvest of stone. Throughout the southern part of the province, stone fences and houses attest to their labour. Failure to clear stones could seriously damage a plough.

Even today, spring is a time when we gather stones. Why? We have a gravel driveway. As a result, every time we use the snowblower to clear the snow, it throws gravel, along with snow, onto our lawn. Add to that the gravel thrown onto the lawn by the giant snowploughs that clear the roads in winter and we are left with a challenging spring task. Failure to clear the lawn of stones results in a very dull lawnmower.

Spring is also a time to clear the flowerbeds of all the debris left behind by winter's retreat: leaves and fallen branches; dead annuals from the year before. It's the season to prune most perennials, cultivate the soil and root out cantankerous crabgrass and weeds. There is a season to plant and a season to uproot.

There's another lesson here. Spring reminds me to cull some of the accumulated junk that clogs the garage, fills my filing cabinets and stuffs the storeroom. It all came to a head when we put our first country home up for sale. I don't want to go through that again! You see, I'm a classic collector, whereas Mary Helen is your model tidy-up-and-get-rid-of it person.

Ever since college, I've collected clippings on every subject imaginable. At first, I very systematically filed them away for later use. Then I became too busy. The result? I had boxes of clippings to file! Plus, I faced the daunting tasks of reducing eight stuffed filing cabinets to two or three, of getting rid of stacks of magazines that I might refer to some day, and of giving away hundreds and hundreds of books that I'll never read.

Add to all this my propensity to hold onto knickknacks from all the places we've visited and to keep shirts and jeans until they totally wear out. I claim to be frugal. Mary Helen claims I cling to stuff. She has, I have to admit, an admirable policy of giving away something every time she buys a new garment.

When I'm honest with myself, I recognize that I'm much too driven by the desire to acquire things, to retain things, to display things. Isn't this, at root, materialism? Jesus warned us, 'Watch out! Be on your guard against all kinds of greed; a man's life does not consist in the abundance of his possessions' (Luke 12:15). He counselled,

Do not store up for yourselves treasures on earth, where moth and rust destroy, and where thieves break in and steal. But store up for yourselves treasures in heaven, where moth and rust do not destroy, and where thieves do not break in and steal. For where your treasure is, there your heart will be also (Matthew 6:19–21).

David, who became quite rich, warned, ' ... though your riches increase, do not set your heart on them' (Psalm 62:10). It's not just those who are rich who endanger their souls, but also those who long to be rich. Paul reminded Timothy about the difference between contentment and discontent—which becomes a drive to acquire wealth:

... godliness with contentment is great gain. For we brought nothing into the world, and we can take nothing out of it. But if we have food and clothing, we will be content with that. People who want to get rich fall into temptation and a trap and into many foolish and harmful desires that plunge men into ruin and destruction. For the love of money is a root of all kinds of evil (1 Timothy 6:6–10).

Wisdom would whisper that spring is not only a time to gather stones and clear debris from the garden, but also to check our garages and closets. Are we accumulating too much stuff? Do we have an acquisitive spirit?

Prayer
Lord, help me to cut down on junk that, like stones, can clutter my life. Deliver me from the desire to collect just for the sake of collecting. Help me to carry around my riches inside, in my mental memory bank. Enrich my soul with thoughts of your triune majesty. Fill me with a sense of the love you displayed on the cross.
Lord, it's not going to be easy because I can justify retaining much of what we have in order to minister more effectively. Since there is some merit in that claim, help me to distinguish what is necessary from what is extraneous. Deliver me from an acquisitive spirit. Amen.

A gloomy day in spring

Bible reading
Psalm 13

Another morning dawns bleak and grey. The fields lie brown and lifeless. Patches of dirty snow linger where earth is still gripped by the now arthritic fingers of retreating winter. Even the evergreens, hardly ever green at the end of a long winter, raise anaemic branches of entreaty to the distant sun. The debris of winter lies everywhere: fallen branches; ruts in the driveway; a piece of wind-blown plastic stuck high in a tree; a beer can lying where it was thrown from a snowmobile. Grubby sand and gravel, left by snowploughs, cakes the roadway. After weeks of clouds, all of nature seems morose.

Inside, driven by routine, I open my Bible, read a few verses—then look away. It seems dry, meaningless. My mood reflects the weather. I just feel listless, gloomy, discouraged. And there seems to be no apparent reason. I have a wife who loves me even when I'm grumpy, and grandchildren who call to ask about our day. Yesterday, I received an encouraging note. I wonder why I don't feel upbeat, cheerful, thankful for the overwhelming goodness of God.

Back to routine. The discipline of devotions. Is this legalism? Hypocrisy? Turning back to Psalm 13 I read, 'How long, O LORD? Will you forget me for ever? How long will you hide your face from me? How long must I wrestle with my thoughts and every day have sorrow in my heart? How long will my enemy triumph over me?' (vv. 1–2).

Now there's something. David had some of the same feelings as I have! True, he had a lot more reason than I do to feel morose. He seemed to have been abandoned by God while his enemies were triumphing.

I read on. 'Look to me and answer, O LORD my God. Give light to my eyes' (v. 3). David prayed for God to send light into the darkness of his soul—a prayer I need to express, and do: 'Lord,' I pray, 'you are a sun and a shield. You give grace and glory [Psalm 84:11]. Please relieve my gloom by the light of your presence. Please shield me from irrational discouragement.'

Nothing happens! I continue to read David's prayer: 'But I trust in your unfailing love; my heart rejoices in your salvation. I will sing to the LORD, for he has been good to me' (vv. 5–6). How could David do that?

David made a choice to trust and to sing. His trust, his joy and his song were rooted in remembering how God had been good to him in the past, days without end. And as I begin to review the wonder of God's gracious salvation, the death of Christ for my sins, the calling of the Holy Spirit to me when I was a rebellious college student, the years and years of protection and provision to this day—I begin to realize that I can trust God even in the gloom.

The sun has not gone anywhere. It is there behind the clouds. A day will come when sunshine banishes the last vestiges of winter. Similarly, God has not gone anywhere, no matter how I feel. He has not changed. He has not abandoned me. He is a sun and a shield. He will give grace and glory, today, tomorrow or the day after. Perhaps I have taken him for granted and failed to worship and adore. If every day was sunny, how would I develop an appreciation for sunshine? If every day my heart was unfailingly cheerful, how would I learn to look beyond my feelings to the unchanging faithfulness of God?

Prayer

Heavenly Father, my feelings are so changeable, so affected by weather and circumstances. Lift up my heart in praise and thanksgiving. Remind me that you are the unchanging bedrock upon which my faith rests. You are the sun beyond the clouds, the rainbow after rain. You are all the blessings that have poured into my life. You are the author of providence, the inspirer of the Scriptures, the sender of angels, the deliverer from temptation. You are hope for an eternal future. I'm already feeling better! Thank you, Lord! Amen.

Giving thanks for green

Bible reading
Psalm 136

Every day I watched for the miracle, the awakening. And then, one day—an April day—I discovered that, overnight, blades of new grass had sprouted and the poplar buds were bursting.

Grey days quickly become magical green days. Every morning became an 'amen' of praise to the divine Artist, a gentle symphony of awakening life heralded by the blush of spreading green. Gentle green. Subtle. Fresh. Vibrant.

Almost overnight, grey was banished from the fields of winter wheat. The ditches came alive with shoots of green. The crocuses flowered. Tulips and daffodils brightened the brown border. Wildflowers rose from the litter. The twigs of all the forest trees, according to a timetable choreographed by the Creator, began to swell and stretch. Slowly, the leaves unfurled and stretched towards the warming sun.

Spring is like a smile, suddenly transforming a face tight with sadness. Or a subtle blush spreading on the face of a young woman at the sight of her beloved.

Every spring, I'm bursting with thankfulness for … green, yes, green, as a pigment, as a symbol of life and hope. What would our world be like without its soothing shades? Yet, in a few short weeks, I forget—I take it for granted, like so much else that comes from the Creator's hand.

Forgive me, Father, for everything I take for granted! And, now that I think of it, what about blue, the colour of sky and water, red, that announces cardinal and rose, orange, the hue of pumpkin and tangerine, and violet, the colour of lilac and amethyst?

If I take colour for granted, what about apples and zebras, bread and butter, coffee and x-rays, dandelions and water? After all, Paul wrote, ' … always giving thanks to God the Father for everything, in the name of our Lord Jesus Christ' (Ephesians 5:20). Clearly, I've got a long way to go before I reach the borders of Thanksgiving Land.

From Philippians, we learn that a dearth of prayer laced with thanksgiving promotes anxiety (4:6). Colossians teaches us that 'overflowing in thankfulness' acts as a catalyst to encourage our growth in Christ (2:7). Colossians also links vigilance to thankfulness (4:2). Failing to 'count our blessings, to name them one by one', makes us careless, spiritually lazy and dangerously naive.

I need to remind myself of David the fugitive, who struggled with fears and failures, the treachery of friends and the power of kingly office. He understood the importance of thanksgiving. He wrote, 'I will give you thanks for ever' (Psalm 30:12). In the Psalms, other authors urge us to 'come before him [the LORD] with thanksgiving'; 'Enter his gates with thanksgiving and his courts with praise; give thanks to him and praise his name'; 'sacrifice thank offerings and tell of his works with songs of joy' (95:2; 100:4; 107:22).

It strikes me that, if I learn to thank God for simple things—all the things I take for granted—I may create a godly habit that will carry me through times of trial like those David suffered. But, even if there is no benefit, I want to be thankful anyway. Without thankfulness, I am blind.

Prayer

And so, Lord, I look out the window and thank you for colour. I look around and thank you for a warm home in winter and a cool home in summer. I thank you for a thoughtful wife, believing children and loving grandchildren. I thank you for the church and for the faith you planted in my heart; for Jesus who loved me so much, he died for me. And I also thank you for daffodils and tulips, pansies and petunias, chickadees and owls, gardens and forests, streams and lakes, sky and sea, sun and stars. Lord, my mouth hangs open as I realize how much there is for which to be thankful. Please, Lord, you know how forgetful I am: remind me often to be thankful. Amen.

april

Dying trees

Bible reading
1 Corinthians 15, especially verses 35–58

I love to wander through our woods in the spring in search of wildflowers. But one spring, I noticed that more trees than usual had died. A pair of aspens had lost the fight. Three of my favourite white pines looked anaemic. My beautiful birch tree had caught birch dieback, and a winter storm had taken down a beech and two cedars.

The spring sun that touches the woods with new life also exposes the presence of sickness and death. Dead and dying trees remind us of our own mortality—something we need to face openly and honestly.

The devil, however, wants to shroud the whole subject in a curtain of dread. Satan holds people 'in slavery by their fear of death' (Hebrews 2:15). The apprehension he exacerbates combines fear of the unknown, worries about a pleasant life coming to an end and melancholy over the thought of separation from friends and family. Add to that the stomach-grabbing alarm we experience at the thought of facing excruciating pain.

To avoid anxiety, we're taught to shun the subject. We let professionals handle the dying and morticians beautify the dead. We surround funerals with flowers and speeches. We talk about the spirit of the dear departed wandering the Elysian Fields.

However, refusal to acknowledge our mortality will not help us live lives of fullness and purpose. Better to face reality. 'There is a time for everything … a time to be born and a time to die … all come from dust, and to dust all return' (Ecclesiastes 3:1–2,20). None of us can know the exact time of our passing. 'Do not boast about tomorrow, for you do not know what a day may bring forth' (Proverbs 27:1). Our lives are in the hand of God.

Of course, if there is no God and we are but the products of evolution—the fateful collision of random molecules—then we need have no fears about death. Atheistic materialists pretend that they can look in the mirror and tell themselves that this life is all there is. And, in preparation for its end, they can agitate for euthanasia to avoid the suffering that might mar their passage into imagined oblivion.

But only the fool denies the existence of God. Instead of fearing death, we should fear the coming judgement. For God 'has set a day when he will judge the world with justice' (Acts 17:31); 'Just as man is destined to die once, and after that to face judgement ... ' (Hebrews 9:27). On that day, 'God will judge men's secrets through Jesus Christ' (Romans 2:16). Those secrets will reveal that all people, without exception, 'have sinned and fall short of the glory of God [God's righteous standards of conduct]' (Romans 3:23).

Jesus warned his hearers often about the destination of unrepentant sinners. Hell is a place where 'their worm does not die and the fire is not quenched' (Mark 9:48). The prospect of being cast into hell is so terrible that Christ said, ' ... if your eye causes you to sin, gouge it out and throw it away. It is better for you to enter life with one eye than to have two eyes and be thrown into the fire of hell' (Matthew 18:9).

In the light of these terrifying truths, how can we face death without debilitating fear? I've taken quite a few funerals and the contrast between those of believers and those arranged for unrepentant men and women is startling.

People who celebrate the home-going of a Christian believer know why genuinely Christian funerals are different. Faith in the saving work of Christ prepares a sinful man or woman to face God's judgement without fear. 'God demonstrates his own love for us in this: While we were still sinners, Christ died for us' (Romans 5:8). Sinners who trust Christ for salvation 'are justified freely by his grace, through the redemption that came by Christ Jesus' (Romans 3:24).

Believers in Jesus Christ die in hope because their sins have been forgiven. They also die in hope because of the transformation they will experience beyond the grave. 'The body that is sown is perishable, it is raised imperishable ... in glory ... in power ... a spiritual body' and immortal (see 1 Corinthians 15:42–55). Jesus Christ takes away the fear of death: 'Death has been swallowed up in victory' (1 Corinthians 15:54). 'Do not let your hearts be troubled. Trust in God; trust also in me. In my

Father's house are many rooms; if it were not so, I would have told you. I am going there to prepare a place for you' (John 14:1–2).

The trees that die in the forest do not die in vain. They decay and fertilize the forest floor, leaving nutrients to feed young saplings. Jesus did not die in vain. His death opens paradise. And those who follow him across the river of death enter heaven leaving behind a heritage of faith and purpose that energizes succeeding generations.

Prayer

Lord, as I age, I admit to some anxiety about my own death—particularly concerning how I will react to pain. I know that it is folly to worry about the future. This is the day you have made—a day of grace in which to celebrate and serve you ... but I'm human, Lord, and weak. Will I persevere in faith to the end? Will I leave a good example to my children and grandchildren? I lay my concerns at your feet. I embrace the cross and pray that you might fill my remaining days with a sense of your presence and love. Help me to love you and worship you all my days. In Jesus' name. Amen.

Resurrection time

Bible reading
John 20:1–18

Spring is resurrection time. Trees, bushes and fields that seemed dead have come alive.

For winter's rains and ruins are over,
And all the season of snows and sins;
The days dividing lover and lover,
The light that loses, the night that wins;
And time remembered is grief forgotten,
And frosts are slain and flowers begotten,
And in green underwood and cover
Blossom by blossom the spring begins.[1]

Wildflowers will soon peek through the warming humus in a race to flower before the forest canopy closes out the warming sun. First, the bloodroot will open its white petals. Then clusters of spring beauties and hepaticas will fringe the forest pathways. Shortly, a carpet of dog-toothed violets will unveil their shy saffron flowers below the maples. The woodlands rise from their wintry rest to don a coat of many colours.

How fitting that we celebrate Easter at this season! On the Friday of Passover, Christ died upon the cross. With his body sealed in a guarded tomb, the enemies of Christ thought that they had triumphed. His disciples retreated behind closed doors to nurse their despair. Satan chortled with glee.

Then, on the first day of the week, Christ arose from death. The women who had witnessed his death and burial came to the tomb to anoint his body with spices. They found the stone rolled away: 'suddenly two men in clothes that gleamed like lightning stood beside them ... "Why do you look for the living among the dead? He is not here; he has risen!"' (Luke 24:1–6).

Up from the grave He arose,
With a mighty triumph o'er His foes;
He arose a Victor from the dark domain,
And He lives forever with His saints to reign,
He arose! He arose! Hallelujah! Christ arose![2]

Overnight, his frightened and despairing disciples became fearless preachers of the gospel. On the day of Pentecost, Peter proclaimed,

Men of Israel, listen to this: Jesus of Nazareth was a man accredited by God to you by miracles, wonders and signs ... you with the help of wicked men, put him to death by nailing him to the cross. But God raised him from the dead, freeing him from the agony of death, because it was impossible for death to keep its hold on him (Acts 2:22–24).

When the religious authorities warned them to stop preaching about Christ, 'Peter and the other apostles replied: "We must obey God rather than men! The God of our fathers raised Jesus from the dead—whom you had killed by hanging him on a tree"' (Acts 5:29–30).

No wonder the apostles refused to compromise their commitment to preach about the risen Christ! Like the spring sun that causes new life to rise from apparently dead soil, Christ raises to spiritual life men and women who are dead to God: 'God, who is rich in mercy, made us alive with Christ even when we were dead in transgressions—it is by grace you have been saved' (Ephesians 2:4–5).

Like the violets and trilliums in our woods that owe their existence to the spring sun, we owe every grace and gift to our risen Christ. No wonder Paul wrote, 'I want to know Christ and the power of his resurrection' (Philippians 3:10)! Peter exulted, 'Praise be to the God and Father of our Lord Jesus Christ! In his great mercy he has given us new birth into a living hope through the resurrection of Jesus Christ from the dead, and into an inheritance that can never perish, spoil or fade—kept in heaven for you' (1 Peter 1:3–4).

Prayer

Heavenly Father, thank you for reflecting the resurrection of your Son in the spring scenes we see around us. It reminds me of the risen power of Jesus Christ, my Lord. Deliver me from living as if the winter of the soul is unending. Touch me daily with the transforming power of resurrection. Amen.

Notes

1 **Algernon Charles Swinburne,** *Atalanta in Calydon*, 1865, stanza 4.
2 **Robert Lowry,** *Christ Arose*.

Watching for signs of spring

Bible reading
Matthew 24:3–14,26–35

In the early months of spring, I keep watch for signs of life. The tiniest indications awaken hope. A swelling bud there, the tip of a tulip here, blades of new grass yonder. After months of snow, ice and chill, the singing season arrives so slowly!

Then, almost overnight, signs appear everywhere. Spring's onset reminds me to watch for the signs of Christ's return. The yearly deliverance of earth from winter's grip mirrors the day when creation will be liberated from its bondage. Jesus said, 'Now learn this lesson from the fig tree: As soon as its twigs get tender and its leaves come out, you know that summer is near. Even so, when you see all these things [signs], you know that it [the coming of the Son of Man] is near, right at the door' (Matthew 24:32–33).

Spring comes every year. We expect it. We watch for the signs of its arrival. But the return of Christ will come suddenly, when we least expect it. He warned, 'Watch out … No one knows about that day or hour … Therefore keep watch … the Son of Man will come at an hour when you do not expect him (vv. 4,36,42,44).

Fortunately, Jesus gave us a list of signs leading up to his return. Wars, famines and earthquakes, 'the beginning of birth pangs', appear with increasing intensity. Twentieth-century wars exceeded the carnage of earlier eras. The dawning of the twenty-first century brought us 9/11 and plunged us into the age of terror. Middle Eastern hatreds appear increasingly intractable. Famine and AIDS destroy Africa. Alarming poverty increases.[1]

Persecution expands: 'you will be handed over to be persecuted and put to death' (v. 9). Researchers tell us that the last century produced more martyrs than at any time in church history. Fanatical Muslims have left in their wake burnt churches and dead Christians in northern Nigeria and Sulawesi. Hindu extremists have burned churches in India. Eritrean authorities have jailed hundreds of Christians, including twenty-eight pastors, many of whom were imprisoned in metal shipping containers. Thousands of Christians have lost their lives in Africa, the Middle East, China, Indonesia and the Central Asian republics.

By contrast, missionary work prospers. Jesus predicted, 'And this gospel of the kingdom will be preached in the whole world as a testimony to all nations, and then the end will come' (v. 14). This prophecy is closer to fulfilment now than at any other era in history. Missiologists have identified almost every unreached people group in the world. As the decades unfold and church-planting teams reach out, the number of unreached groups declines and the return of Christ draws ever closer.

Fulfilling another prediction, the Christian faith is under increasing attack. Movies and novels spread misinformation and prejudice against the biblical faith. Pseudo-scientific studies seek to trace religious faith to human DNA. Ponder the unbelievable resilience of evolution as a theory of everything—despite lack of evidence. Note Richard Dawkins' vitriolic polemic, *The God Delusion*. Consider the resurgence of Hinduism, Buddhism and especially Islam, along with the spread of cults of every kind.

Despite persecution and prejudice, the church of Jesus Christ grows. And yet, as predicted, 'the love of most' grows cold. Too many professing Christians now accept as normative divorce, adultery, homosexuality, termination of pregnancies, premarital sex, dishonesty and debt. Christians have lost the moral high-ground, especially in Western nations.

Further, Christ warns of the rise of 'false Christs and false prophets [who] will appear and perform great signs and miracles to deceive even the elect—if that were possible' (v. 24). Attempts to draw up a list of false prophets would exhaust this whole book.

But wait, you say, signs like these have always been present. You are right. Believers in the first century saw many of these signs. So did Christians in the Middle Ages. However, in our day, their intensity and worldwide prevalence appear to be on the ascendancy. Earthquakes, such as the one that led to the Asian tsunami, tend to be worse. Hurricanes, cyclones and tornadoes seem more catastrophic; drought and wildfires more intense; persecution more widespread and deadly.

As already noted, one sign that Christ's return is closer to fulfilment than at any time in history—the preaching of the gospel to every ethnic group. Until modern times, the Americas and the islands of the sea were beyond the reach of missionaries. Before the Iron Curtain fell, the communist world, including the vast reaches of Central and East Asia, was largely closed. Inaccessible countries and unreachable peoples dotted the earth. Today, the gospel, through radio, TV and the Internet, is touching people everywhere. Missionary teams dedicated to almost every people group either already exist or are in the planning stage.

We would be very unwise to be complacent and assume that Christ's return is distant. 'No one knows about that day or hour ... therefore keep watch ... because the Son of Man will come at an hour when you do not expect him' (vv. 36,42,44). As surely as spring arrives each year, Christ will return. Even so, come Lord Jesus!

Prayer
Lord, I do yearn for your coming, yet I admit that this hope is often far from my thoughts. Deliver me from complacency, carelessness and unfaithfulness. Help me to keep watching, keep praying and keep working to extend your kingdom. Remind me to keep looking forward to the day when you will come on the clouds of glory. There is so much evil and injustice on earth; so much violence and cruelty. And your children face such terrible persecution in countries like Iran, Turkmenistan and Saudi Arabia. And, Master, so many of our churches seem to have drifted from a focus on your commission. Holy Spirit, revive us. Father, speed the gospel to the last tribe. Jesus, please hasten your return! Amen.

Notes

1 Matthew 24, like many prophetic passages, has a double fulfilment. Woven through the passage are the answers to two questions from the disciples: 'When will this happen?', meaning the destruction of the temple and Jerusalem, and 'What will be the sign of your coming and of the end of the age?' (v. 3).

When last year's leaves hang on

Bible reading
Ephesians 4:17–32

S ome trees hardly seem ready for their new spring clothing. At the onset of winter, the maples and birches, the walnuts and poplars shed their leaves, adding to the rich humus on the forest floor. Beneath this blanket, the wildflowers await the warming sun. The white oak and beech, however, have stubbornly refused to give up their leaves so easily. Clad in their brown rags, they have defiantly resisted the wildest efforts of the wind to disrobe them.

Only the onset of spring can send their leaves floating to earth. The sun shines brighter. Temperatures rise. Sap swells the buds on the end of each twig, tickling the nascent leaves into growth. The unfurling new leaves dislodge the old.

Spurgeon, a great nineteenth-century preacher, wrote,

Neither frost nor wind has removed the withered foliage, but the spring has soon made a clearance. The new life dislodges the old, pushing it away as unsuitable to it. So our old corruptions are best removed by the growth of new graces. 'Old things are passed away; behold all things are become new.' It is as the new life buds and opens that the old worn-out things of our former state are compelled to quit their hold on us ... the new leaves of grace pushing off our old sere affections and habits of sin ... With converts from the world it is often better not to lay down stringent rules as to worldly amusements, but leave the new life and its holier joys to push off the old pleasures. Thus it will be done more naturally and more effectively.[1]

Our passage in Ephesians exhorts us 'to be made new in the attitude of your minds; and to put on the new self, created to be like God in true righteousness and holiness' (vv. 23–24). Following this exhortation, Paul gives examples of the replacement principle. Like new growth on an oak tree, honest speech is to displace falsehood, forgiveness is to smother anger, honest work is to replace stealing and words that build others up are to banish unwholesome talk.

This principle certainly applies to the crucial replacement of outright sin with that which is good and true. There can be no compromise here. But, too often, we fail to carry the principle over into other more innocent but more morally debatable areas of our lives: our reading material; the TV programmes we watch; the hobbies we embrace; the vacations we take; the kinds of foods we eat; the sedentary way in which we spend our days; care in spending our money.

As we mature in Christ, we will want to replace old habits that may not be bad, or even especially harmful, with new practices that surpass these in excellence. We will desire to replace the good with the better and the better with the best. For example, who can deny that we should replace the use of copious quantities of sugar, salt and fat with more healthy alternatives?

As soon as I broach this subject, I realize how easy it is to fall into legalism; to craft a bunch of rules that we may try to foist on others. We must flee this danger. The gospel brings freedom.

The replacement principle—replacing neutral patterns with more excellent choices—will mean different things to different people. To one person, it may mean reducing TV viewing to make time for devotional or theological reading. To another, it might mean watching more TV and reading less theology, in order to gain an understanding of how to communicate the gospel to this generation. To one, it might mean talking less and listening more. To another, it might mean breaking shy silence to speak out more. It might lead the workaholic to spend more quality time with spouse and family. Growth in Christ includes replacing something that is not evil in itself with an attitude or activity that glorifies God more fully.

Prayer
Lord, as I think of my life, replacement means replacing critical comments with words that edify. It means I need to eat more fruits and vegetables. It means that I need to set aside more time

for prayer as well as more time for hobbies. It means that I need to be more concerned about fulfilling the ministry you have given me than about pleasing others by doing what others think I should do. And learning to say no graciously. And, Lord, I'm sure it means less time in front of the TV. Grant discernment, I pray, so that I may do what is excellent rather than what is merely allowable. Amen.

Notes

1 **C. H. Spurgeon,** *Flowers From a Puritan's Garden* (Harrisburg, VA: Sprinkle Publications, 1976), p. 97.

may

Same old, same old

Bible reading
Psalm 148

In my childhood, meals were predictable. Meat, potatoes and some vegetable, usually carrots, cabbage or turnips during the off season. Spring brought immediate relief to our jaded palates. But today, we can get almost anything we crave at any time of the year, as long as we don't mind the price.

Food pours into our supermarkets from Mexico, Peru, California and South Africa. So in January, when stores began to feature asparagus from Peru, we rejoiced. We love asparagus. Unfortunately, when the local variety became available, we had already become tired of it.

It's easy to get bored eating the same thing day after day. I sympathize with the Israelites who got tired of eating manna in the wilderness. Yet God condemned them for their grumbling. I've always been puzzled by this. Even though the manna 'tasted like wafers made with honey' (Exodus 16:31) or 'something made with olive oil' (Numbers 11:8), a steady diet of manna for forty years must have been enormously frustrating. Of course, they could boil it, bake it, fry it and sauté it. They could add spices. Perhaps having jaded palates was part of their punishment. After all, they rejected a shortcut to the promised land and its culinary abundance.

Nevertheless, I can understand their feelings as captured by Moses in his record: 'We remember the fish we ate in Egypt at no cost—also the cucumbers, melons, leeks, onions and garlic. But now we have lost our appetite; we never see anything but this manna!' (Numbers 11:5–6).

I'll ask the Lord to interpret that passage when I get to heaven. In the meantime, I'll enjoy a world that throbs with diversity—not just in foodstuffs. Butterflies and hummingbirds; kangaroos and camels; potatoes and spinach; mountains and oceans; diamonds and coal; olives and apples: such a multiplicity of shapes, colours and designs. Some display an obvious purpose, but all reflect the Creator's love of variety.

In creation, diversity triumphs. I realize that we feel safe and comfortable in familiar places, doing predictable things according to a set schedule. But shouldn't we break out of the mould occasionally? Imitate the Creator? Why, then, does diversity flourish everywhere in our world except in our social circles? Why do we expect neighbours, friends and children to conform to our image of normality? Wearing the same clothes. Speaking the same language. Living in similar houses. Painted the same colours. Having identical lawns. Interested in the same things. Liking the same music. Eating the same foods. Reading the same books.

Unless we regularly shake ourselves out of a rut, we tend to become narrow, legalistic and boring. I can't imagine God, the architect of variety, rubber-stamping our attempts to domesticate creativity. Or are we punishing ourselves, as God did the rebellious Israelites?

If God is the author of variety—and he is—our lives and churches should encourage creativity. Uplifting music. Thoughtful poetry and prose. Attractive architecture. Beautiful gardens. Inspiring art. Interesting and challenging sermons. Creative outreach programmes.

Why do we try to force multiplicity into one-size-fits-all programmes? Too often, we cling to mono-cultural traditions about dress, music, schedules and social mores that have nothing to do with biblical truth. They are simply cultural customs developed during a particular time in history. Preferences are fine, but hollow traditions can be deadening. Indeed, enforced conformity is poisonous to the human soul.

Surely our local churches, as part of the church universal, should celebrate diversity. That includes ethnic diversity. Hasn't Christ called us to himself from thousands of languages and races? Like a jeweller crafting settings for rubies and sapphires and diamonds and turquoise, God created the church to be a place where each person can hone his or her gifts until they shine—no matter what the ethnic background. When it happens, we should rejoice. When it doesn't, we drone on—and on and on. But who am I to talk? I get into a rut so easily.

Prayer

Heavenly Father, too often I wake up to realize I'm in a rut. A comfortable rut. Help me to bring some variety into my life. Lord, I don't have trouble with variety in the garden or on the table. But forgive me for falling into mind-numbing sameness in my devotions and prayer life. Keep me from being unbiblically critical of diversity in music and ministry. Help our church to embrace the right kind of diversity—not change for the sake of change, but change that demonstrates vibrant life. Arouse in us all a new creative impulse. Amen.

The miracle of a leaf

Bible reading
Luke 6:27–36

All along the valley and over the hills, the first flush of spring green began to transform the drab grey and worn-out brown garments of winter. The unfolding of a million billion leaves wrought the change. And each leaf was a miracle.

Mark Buchanan has written,

A leaf. Behold a single leaf … Hold it open in your palm. It is perfect as a newborn's smile. Pinch its stem between thumb and forefinger and hold it to the light. Eden bleeds through. Its veins are like bone work in silhouette. This single leaf, joined to the tree, drinks poison from the air, drinks it serenely as Socrates downing his cup of hemlock, and refuses to return in kind, instead spilling out life-giving oxygen. This leaf tilts to catch the sun, its warmth and radiance, to distill the heat and light down to the shadow, down to the roots, back up to limbs. To shade the earth. To feed you and me.[1]

A lesson from a leaf! Instead of spewing out carbon monoxide, deadly sulphur vapour or some other noxious compound, leaves turn toxins into oxygen and food. If only we could learn to do the same.

Jesus taught us, 'Love your enemies, do good to those who hate you, bless those who curse you, pray for those who mistreat you … Be merciful, just as your Father is merciful' (Luke 6:27–28,36). As the Father allows his sun to shine on the just and the unjust, his rain to fall on all, his good gifts to be showered indiscriminately, so we are to transform hatred and cursing and mistreatment into deeds of love and blessing. Instead of seeking justice, plotting revenge, drawing away from those who mistreat us, we are to return to our tormentors that which they could never imagine.

As if those few verses are not enough, Jesus goes on to hammer home this revolutionary principle: 'If someone strikes you on one cheek, turn to him the other also. If someone takes your cloak, do not stop him from taking your tunic … if anyone takes what belongs to you, do not demand it back' (vv. 29–30).

Lord, that's tough. How can I wave good morning to the neighbour who has ruined my lawnmower? How can I forgive the thoughtless person? How can I be loving when I'm so carelessly misunderstood? Won't I perpetuate an injustice? Aren't I setting myself up for more abuse? Won't I project the image of being a pushover? Lord, it's so unnatural.

I guess that's the point. The kingdom of God is not about acting like everyone else. Jesus taught, 'If you love those who love you, what credit is that to you? Even "sinners" love those who love them. And if you do good to those who are good to you, what credit is that to you? Even "sinners" do that?' (vv. 32–33).

Jesus had in mind overturning the natural order, instituting a revolutionary response to others by returning good for evil. And yet, I seem socialized to limit my responses to returning good for good. To invite someone for dinner who has previously invited us. To send a card to those who sent cards to us in a similar situation. To say 'good morning' to those who reciprocate. To help those who are grateful. Christ calls me to move it up a notch: to send cards to those who will never reciprocate, casseroles to those who have been miserable neighbours and phone calls to those who never phone us. (Incidentally, when I mention neighbours, I'm talking generally. We've had wonderful neighbours.)

Responding to people as Jesus directs requires a supernatural reordering of our lives. No wonder we need the minute-by-minute empowering of the Holy Spirit!

Imagine if every Christian, like every leaf, returned good for evil: drivers refused to blow their horns in frustration at those who cut in front of them; neighbours kept on loaning their tools even when they came back damaged; Christians kept on praying for columnists who deny Christ; parents continued to love rebellious children; grown-up children forgave workaholic parents for neglect … What a difference we would make! The light of Christ's love would shine brighter and farther.

Prayer

Lord, help me to embrace the principles of your kingdom by responding as you did to those who spitefully used you. Enable me to overcome the anger and annoyance that arises from rudeness, ill treatment or being ignored. Inspire me to go about doing good, speaking words of encouragement and smiling. May I be one who loves to do random acts of kindness. Amen.

Notes

1 **Mark Buchanan,** *The Holy Wild* (Sisters, OR: Multnomah, 2003), p. 53.

A stinging spring day

Bible reading
Genesis 3:1–19

I was merrily doing my spring thing—weeding and cultivating the flower beds—when, suddenly, my left hand began to tingle and burn. Looking down, I realized I had grubbed a stinging nettle out of the soil with my bare hand. I tend to weed at full speed, rooting out weeds with my left hand while I cultivate with the trowel in my right hand. I've tried working with gloves but I can't get the feel of the soil or enough of a grip on weeds. Clearly, my approach misses in care what it makes up for in speed.

For the rest of the day, I paid for my carelessness with a burning sensation that nothing would alleviate. When the fingers on my left hand stopped burning, the hand felt numb.

My nettle experience was a painful reminder that we live in a fallen world. As a consequence of Adam's sin, God declared, 'Cursed is the ground because of you; through painful toil you will eat of it … It will produce thorns and thistles for you' (Genesis 3:17–18). To keep the garden free of weeds and nettles, I must labour long and hard. My lawn has too little grass and too many weeds. My garden has too much grass. Work that out.

Dirty, cracked fingernails; sweat; aching muscles: the path to a beautiful flower garden and flourishing vegetables is an uphill struggle. So much of the natural world reflects the beauty of its Creator, but experience warns me about the poison ivy waiting to blister my skin and the mosquitoes thirsty for my blood.

Sin entered the Garden of Eden, and every garden since has borne in its soil the seeds of its own destruction. Whenever a gardener eases up, weeds and bugs threaten to take over.

And what is true in the natural world is certainly true among the children of Adam. God warned Cain, 'If you do what is right, will you not be accepted? But if you do not do what is right, sin is crouching at your door; it desires to have you, but you must master it' (Genesis 4:7). Cain let down his guard. Sin slew his constraint and he slew Abel, his brother.

From that time to this, we have had dysfunctional families, dishonest merchants, corrupt politicians and scheming dictators—plus so much more: ravenous lions and poisonous snakes; rabid dogs and ferocious microbes; murder; robbery; abuse; deceit; pride; envy; slavery; prostitution; pornography; cancer; AIDS; heart disease; sickness; despair; death.

And the bad is not all out there in the larger world among other people, or in our garden: it's in our own hearts. We're fallen, sinful creatures. Unconsciously, we often choose the selfish, the proud, the hurtful way. If the great apostle Paul could cry, 'I know that nothing good lives in me, that is, in my sinful nature' (Romans 7:18), and David, 'I know my transgressions, and my sin is always before me' (Psalm 51:3), then who are we to deny what we are? ' ... for all have sinned and fall short of the glory of God' (Romans 3:23).

The most foolish—and the most dangerous—thing we can do is deny the reality of evil. The first principle the Lord Jesus taught his disciples concerned the blessedness of those who are poor in spirit (the first Beatitude, Matthew 5:3); that is, those who are humble and honest about their spiritual poverty. Pride blinds. Humility illumines the soul, both to its own baser instincts and to the glories of God. The second principle of the King concerns the blessedness of those who maintain an attitude of revulsion towards sin—they mourn (the second Beatitude, Matthew 5:4). They are comforted by receiving God's forgiveness, but they never take this for granted. They don't call a truce with unrighteousness; it is always their enemy.

Obviously, this world is not paradise, nor is it our ultimate home. Its most beautiful gardens are not the Garden by the River. There will be a new heaven and a new earth in which dwells righteousness—and flowers and fruitful trees. There will be no pain or tears there, no death. I doubt if there will be stinging nettles or poison ivy in that garden, either.

Meanwhile, we must keep down the weeds if we are to harvest a crop. We must attack the noxious attitudes of selfishness and arrogance with the spade of confession and the fire of repentance. We must look to heaven in prayer for the refreshing rain of the Spirit to produce in us the fruits of righteousness. We must long for the Sun of Righteousness to cast his light upon us that we might grow.

Prayer

Father, help me to live under the shadow of the cross, for I am a sinner. Show me my sins—but not all at once, lest I be overwhelmed. Forgive me, but don't let me take the cleansing blood of Christ for granted. May I be truly sorrowful, but not so overcome that I sink in despair. Gracious Lord, help me to live every day in dependence upon your transforming power. When I see evil in the world around me, or in my own heart, or in the lives of family or friends, help me to remember the victory that Christ won. Give me patience to wait for your ultimate triumph over all evil. As I am forgiven, help me to be forgiving. In Jesus' name. Amen.

Honey in a wounded giant

Bible reading
2 Corinthians 1:3–11

Century-old white pines guarded the country lane where we used to walk. I loved the profile of those forest giants. Unfortunately, their height courted lightning. Wild summer storms severely blasted two of them. One stood stark and dead against the sky, the other was reduced to a fifty-foot stub, broken off halfway down its trunk.

The hum of swarming bees drew my attention to a huge knothole in the stub. A steady stream of honey bees flew in and out, storing spring's nectar. The lightning that shattered the forest giant had prepared a repository for honey, one of nature's greatest boons.

How can good come from bad, growth from disease, life from death? How can tragedy prepare for triumph? High on the list of those perennial mysteries we ponder is this one: the mystery of suffering.

God assures believers that good will triumph in their lives: 'We know that in all things God works for the good of those who love him, who have been called according to his purpose' (Romans 8:28). Sometimes, the way we use this verse seems more like that of a mantra than an article of practical faith.

Consider Job—a scary proposition! Could these kinds of tragedies happen in my life? Yet this story of suffering has a wonderful finale. At the end of his trials, Job testified, 'My ears had heard of you but now my eyes have seen you. Therefore I despise myself and repent in dust and ashes' (Job 42:5–6). Subsequently, Job was 'comforted and consoled … [and the] LORD blessed the latter part of Job's life more than the first' (vv. 11–12).

Job's experience has been duplicated throughout history. From prison, Paul wrote to the Philippians, 'what has happened to me has really served to advance the gospel. As a result, it has become clear throughout the whole palace guard and to everyone else that I am in chains for Christ' (Philippians 1:12–13). Because of his imprisonment, 'most of the brothers in the Lord have been encouraged to speak the word of God more courageously and fearlessly' (v. 14).

Second Corinthians records how Paul learned of God's power in the crucible of suffering:

But we have this treasure [the glory of God in the face of Christ] in jars of clay to show that this all-surpassing power is from God and not from us. We are hard pressed on every side, but not crushed; perplexed, but not in despair; persecuted, but not abandoned; struck down, but not destroyed. We always carry around in our body the death of Jesus, so that the life of Jesus may also be revealed in our body (2 Corinthians 4:7–10).

These biblical precedents sometimes seem alien to our modern context. To understand how tribulation can metaphorically produce honey, we need to see God at work in our own era. Fortunately, when I listen to a seasoned saint reflect on trials, the comments I hear are usually positive. They tell of lessons learned, how they have grown and how they treasure their closer relationship to God.

After Joni Eareckson Tada broke her neck in a diving accident, she founded Joni and Friends. This ministry has brought help to multitudes around the world through their daily radio programmes and by supplying 25,000 wheelchairs to developing countries. She writes, 'I am convinced that the whole ordeal of my paralysis was inspired by God's love. I wasn't the brunt of some cruel divine joke. God had reasons behind my suffering, and learning some of them has made all the difference in the world.'[1]

How God distils good from evil is still puzzling—until God brings trials into our own lives. We are such slow learners, a fact compounded by the media's message that pleasure, good health and abundant provision are our inalienable rights. Spiritual realities seem so ethereal.

Admittedly, I'm a particularly slow learner. It took multiplied trials as a missionary in Pakistan to convince me of the reality of Jesus' promise, 'I am with you always' (Matthew 28:20). It took decades of financial crises for me to learn that 'my God will meet all your needs according to his glorious riches in Christ Jesus' (Philippians 4:19). Through years of teaching and preaching—which I never found easy—I kept relearning that 'I can do everything through him who gives me strength' (Philippians 4:13).

I still needed to learn empathy for those in physical distress. I always walked fast, loved to hike and hated hospitals! Then came shortness of breath and restricted activity. After a series of tests, the diagnosis of severe heart blockage with no surgical options came as a blow.

Why, Lord? His answer seemed to be, 'You need to learn that I am "The God of all comfort, who comforts us in all our troubles, so that we can comfort those in any trouble with the comfort we ourselves have received from God" [2 Corinthians 1:3–4].' I'm slowly learning to have more compassion—and that's good. And I have much more appreciation for health-care professionals—that's good too, like honey in that lightning-blasted pine.

Prayer

Lord, help me to be more compassionate and comforting to others who face severe trials. Help me to value your care and comfort more than any creature comfort. But, if it is your will, help me to learn more of faith and hope and love and patience and joy and peace without having to go through trials to see their value. If it is your will, help me to maintain a measure of health and strength, that I might serve you all my days. Amen.

Notes

1 Quoted in **John Blanchard,** *Where is God When Things Go Wrong?* (Darlington: Evangelical Press, 2005), p. 37.

The wind

Bible reading
Romans 8:1–17

Weather permitting, Mary Helen and I like to take a morning walk. After checking the thermometer, I scan the trees outside for some indication of the strength of the wind. If it's a hot day, a breeze will make it tolerable, but during a cold snap, a stiff wind will make the wind chill unbearable.

Most days, we take the wind for granted. Even though meteorologists include wind speed in their forecasts, it doesn't make much impact on us, unless they warn of damaging winds. Usually we're more interested in whether the day will be sunny or overcast, rainy or foggy, warm or cold. But without wind, life would be miserable. We'd bake in the sun with no wind to bring clouds to shade us, or freeze without wind to drive the clouds away on cold days. Wind evaporates the water to make rain and snow, and moves moisture around the earth. Without wind, fog shuts down airports and snarls up traffic.

The way we often take the Holy Spirit for granted resembles how we overlook the importance of the wind. A Pharisee named Nicodemus came to Jesus by night to escape the notice of his fellow religionists. When Jesus informed him of his need to be born again by the Spirit, Nicodemus was astonished. 'How can a man be born when he is old?' he asked. Jesus replied, 'Flesh gives birth to flesh [the first birth], but the Spirit gives birth to spirit [spiritual rebirth] … "You must be born again." The wind blows wherever it pleases. You hear its sound, but you cannot tell where it comes from or where it is going. So it is with everyone born of the Spirit' (John 3:1–8).

The work of the Spirit is as mysterious and invisible as the wind. The only way I can tell if the wind is blowing is by looking out of my window to see if tree branches are moving. And we can only tell that the Spirit has been at work by looking around for evidences of his influence. Have people who were previously careless about sin been convicted of their need of salvation? Then the Spirit has been blowing through their hearts. 'When he [the Spirit] comes, he will convict the world of guilt in regard to sin and righteousness and judgment' (John 16:8).

Have unbelievers come to faith? Then the Holy Spirit has been at work. Jesus asserted to Nicodemus, 'whoever believes in him [Christ] shall not perish but have eternal life' (John 3:16).

Have people who were agnostics, atheists or just indifferent begun to declare that God is their Father? Then the Spirit has been acting: 'by him [the Spirit] we cry, "Abba, Father"' (Romans 8:15).

Have those who were ignorant of, or even antagonistic towards, the Scriptures begun to love and understand God's Word? Then we can be sure that the great interpreter of Scripture has been moving through their hearts: 'when he, the Spirit of truth, comes, he will guide you into all truth' (John 16:13).

Do you see changes for good in those who once were blasphemers, immoral, dishonest and selfish? Then we know that the Holy Spirit has begun to produce the good fruit of righteousness in them: 'the fruit of the Spirit is love, joy, peace, patience, kindness, goodness, faithfulness, gentleness and self-control' (Galatians 5:22–23).

Have insecure, anxious and doubtful people become confident of God's love and their own salvation? Ah, then, the Spirit of adoption has been whispering in their hearts: 'you did not receive a spirit that makes you a slave again to fear, but you received the Spirit of sonship ... The Spirit himself testifies with our spirit that we are God's children' (Romans 8:15–16).

Life on earth without the presence of the wind is unthinkable; spiritual life without the influence of the Holy Spirit is unimaginable: 'when the kindness and love of God our Saviour appeared, he saved us, not because of righteous things we had done, but because of his mercy. He saved us through the washing of rebirth and renewal by the Holy Spirit, whom he poured out on us generously through Jesus Christ our Saviour' (Titus 3:4–6).

Prayer

Blessed Holy Spirit, I'm so very thankful for your influences on my life: convicting me of rebellion and sin; moving me to faith in Jesus Christ; delivering me from bondage to sin and wooing me back into the forgiving arms of Jesus when I fall; opening the Scriptures to my understanding and delight; assuring me that I am a child of the Father; leading me into fellowship with other believers; producing in me qualities that are contrary to my fallen nature; gifting me, like every other believer, for some kingdom ministry; giving me hope when I despair and strength when I'm tempted.

Spirit of the living God, how manifold is your benevolence! Forgive me when I take you for granted. Remind me every day of your quiet presence. Accept my worship and thanksgiving. Amen.

june

Waves

Bible reading
Psalm 93

Occasionally, I entertain a tiny regret that we don't own a house by the water. I breathe a prayer: 'Lord, I don't think this is covetousness—is it? Just a longing. It wouldn't really matter whether it was on a lake or at the ocean, or even on a hill with a sweeping view of a watery horizon. OK, I know I'm being unreasonable.'

Prices show that everyone else seems to have the same dream. Fortunately, we live within a few miles of the shore of Lake Ontario, a lake so large as to be almost an inland sea. We often put together a picnic and drive down to Presqu'ile Park, where we claim a picnic table and then— well—just relax. Depending on the weather, we may sit and watch the waves gently lap the shore or froth and foam in a disciplined uproar of sound and fury. Sometimes we meander along the beach, picking up the odd shell, pebble, bit of polished glass or unusual piece of driftwood. Often we watch gulls and terns dive and wheel. But usually, we'll just let the rhythm of the waves wash over us in soothing ripples of sound.

An informal survey I've conducted over the years seems to indicate that expanses of water captivate all kinds of people. At every beach I've ever visited, people sit or stand facing the water. I've never yet seen anyone with his or her back to the ocean—except momentarily. Even sunbathers lie where they can peek at the water from time to time. Water that stretches towards the horizon exerts a mysterious power.

Water's fascination is not completely explained by the opportunity it affords to swim, boat, fish or snorkel; no, it speaks to us of something more elemental and seemingly infinite. Great expanses of water, particularly the ocean, speak to me of God: 'The sea is his, for he made it' (Psalm 95:5). They illustrate the unfathomable greatness of God who alone 'treads on the waves of the sea' (Job 9:8).

The immensity of the ocean can make us feel like an ant climbing Mount Everest. It stretches from horizon to horizon. It circles the earth. It plunges into depths unexplored by mankind. 'Great is the LORD and most worthy of praise; his greatness no one can fathom' (Psalm 145:3).

We clear the forests and plough the fields and carve out roads, but no one can either tame the sea or domesticate the Almighty. The Lord reminded Job of this reality: 'Who shut up the sea behind doors when it burst forth from the womb, when I made the clouds its garment and wrapped it in thick darkness, when I fixed limits for it and set its doors and bars in place, when I said, "This far you may come and no farther; here is where your proud waves halt"?' (Job 38:8–11).

God alone can tame the unruly waves of the sea: 'O LORD God Almighty, who is like you? ... You rule over the surging sea; when its waves mount up, you still them' (Psalm 89:8–9). The Lord of the sea is Lord of all, the sovereign ruler of the universe whose authority and power tower above our petty rivalries and political manoeuvrings. He, and no other, can solve our national dilemmas, dispel our personal despair and soothe our troubled hearts.

The waves of the sea murmur incessantly about the irresistible power of God: 'The seas have lifted up, O LORD, the seas have lifted up their voice' (Psalm 93:3). No diver beneath the surface of the sea can ignore its laws. No sea coast can ignore the sea's anger. No ship may sail its expanse without submission to its rules. But infinitely greater than the force of the sea is the might of God: 'Mightier than the thunder of the great waters, mightier than the breakers of the sea—the LORD on high is mighty' (Psalm 93:4).

The sea speaks of mystery, not only from its unreachable depths but also along every shore. There are shells to discover: what creature inhabited this spiral palace? Driftwood to examine: how many waves did it take to transform this into an octopus? A myriad of coloured pebbles to inspect: how many centuries did it take to round their fractured edges? Perhaps a nugget or two of coloured glass—amber, jade or diamond: what could be their provenance? A bit of sculpted wood: which schooner lost a spar? Like the mysterious sea, 'How unsearchable [are] his [God's] judgments, and his paths beyond tracing out! Who has known the mind of the Lord? Or who has been his counsellor?' (Romans 11:33–34).

So we finish our picnic, lean back and let the soothing sound of waves lapping on the shore do their work. Sometimes we pick up a book. Sometimes—I hope more and more often—we let the waves remind us of the greatness of our Lord: infinite in power; mysterious and unsearchable in glory; sovereign in authority. 'Oh, the depth of the riches of the wisdom and knowledge of God! ... For from him and through him and to him are all things. To him be the glory for ever! Amen' (Romans 11:33,36).

Prayer
Father, Son and Holy Spirit, I bow before you. When troubles overwhelm me, the future seems bleak or events spiral out of control, remind me of waves on the sea. Father, fill me with awe as I contemplate again your infinite power and sovereign authority. Lord Jesus, you who stilled the sea and walked on water, calm my anxious fears and help me to walk with you, hand in hand. Wind of the Spirit, blow through my life in refreshing power. Amen.

That bitter root

Bible reading
Ephesians 4:25–32

One year, I constructed a ten- by four-foot raised vegetable plot in a shabby section of our lawn. Since the soil was sandy, the task seemed laughably simple. Hah! I encountered roots that went deep and spread everywhere. Removing the soil and straining out every root fragment took a week of spare time.

The author of Hebrews used roots as a metaphor for bitterness: 'See to it that … no bitter root grows up to cause trouble and defile many' (Hebrews 12:15). Bitterness is a deep-seated, often unconscious attitude that sends up harmful thoughts at unpredictable intervals.

While reading a magazine the other day, a flash of resentment surfaced about something that happened twenty-five years ago. Why would such an irrational thought pop up so unpredictably? Hadn't I dealt with that decades ago? The roots must be deeper than I thought.

Bitterness is ubiquitous: victims of crime, labourers treated poorly by contractors, homebound wives unappreciated by their husbands, indigenous tribes neglected by governments, children of absentee parents, cancer sufferers. Some parents even feel bitter about a child whose birth curtailed their freedoms. Bitterness can choke friendships, ruin family relationships and strangle churches. Harbouring bitterness is like swallowing a slow-acting and deadly poison.

James dramatically explains its origin: 'What causes fights and quarrels among you? Don't they come from your desires that battle within you? You want something but don't get it. You kill and covet, but you cannot have what you want. You quarrel and fight' (James 4:1–2).

Let me clarify: we all have desires. Some are normal but others arise from wrong motives—desires that balloon into lusts. Anger arises when something or someone blocks our desires, keeping us from getting what we want. Anger often spawns a quarrel, which may spiral out of control into a shouting match, a physical fight or—in extreme cases—murder. Anger held inside and not dealt with produces resentment. Over time, resentment develops into bitterness.

Notice the connection between bitterness, anger, conflict and slander in the following verse: 'Get rid of all bitterness, rage and anger, brawling and slander, along with every form of malice' (Ephesians 4:31). The Scriptures often connect these attitudes and actions (see Romans 1:26; 2 Corinthians 12:20; Galatians 5:20–21).

We can keep bitterness from taking root by rejecting feelings of resentment towards others the moment they arise. At the onset of such a feeling, we need to confess it to God and ask him to replace it with love. If we expressed our resentment openly in words or actions, we should ask forgiveness of the person who was our target. On the other hand, if we became the target of another's anger, we still have a responsibility to seek reconciliation and express forgiveness.

Genuine Christians are commanded to forgive others as Christ forgave us: 'Be kind and compassionate to one another, forgiving each other, just as in Christ God forgave you' (Ephesians 4:32).

What do we do if bitterness has sunk roots deep into our psyches? Like the weeds in my garden, deep-rooted resentments are hard to eradicate. They require the radical help that only the Holy Spirit can give—over a period of time.

Corrie Ten Boom suffered under the Nazis during the Second World War. She struggled to forget a wrong. She had forgiven the person, but kept thinking about the incident at night. After two sleepless weeks, she cried out to God for help. Help came in the form of a kindly Lutheran pastor. When she related her problem to him, he pointed to a bell tower. He explained that, after the sexton let go of the bell rope, the bell would keep on swinging—DING, DONG, DINg, Dong, d-i-n-g. The notes would get slower and slower and quieter and quieter until finally, with a last ding, the sound stopped.

He said, 'I believe it is the same with forgiveness—when we forgive we let go the rope, but if we've been tugging at our grievances for a long time, we mustn't be surprised if the old angry thoughts keep coming for a while. They're just the ding dongs of the old bell slowing down.'[1]

And so it proved to be with Corrie. She felt a few more midnight reverberations and a couple of 'dings' when the subject came up in conversations. But the force of the anger dissipated as Corrie's willingness to hang on to the matter disappeared. The memories finally faded. The root of bitterness had been eradicated.

By an act of the will, we must choose to let go of the bell rope of bitterness the moment a bitter thought arises. Sweet forgetfulness will gradually overpower the bitter memories and suffuse our lives with tenderness towards others. (This devotional barely touches this vast and very important subject. For a fuller treatment, read my book *The Guide: Revolutionary Forgiveness.*[2])

Prayer

Lord Jesus, since you were tempted in all points like us, you must have dealt with anger. Help me to follow your lead and become a forgiving person. Enable me to deal lovingly with people who knowingly or unknowingly hurt me. Keep resentments from festering. Root out every form of bitterness. Lord, please suppress all those imaginary slights that I tend to nurture. And, yes, I have to admit that I sin against others. Give me the courage to go to those I hurt to ask for their forgiveness. Help me to deal with anger every day before the sun goes down. Amen.

Notes

1   Quoted in **R. David Roberts,** *Forgiveness* (Wheaton, IL: Leadership, 1987), p. 48.

2   **Eric E. Wright,** *The Guide: Revolutionary Forgiveness* (Darlington: Evangelical Press, 2002).

Faith and sunshine

Bible reading
Ephesians 2:1–10

The worries of hobby gardeners like me are minor compared with the anxieties of farmers. Often on the brink of bankruptcy, they depend on the right balance of sunshine and rain for their livelihoods.

Although not in their league, I anxiously watch the thermometer during the early spring. Will an overnight freeze kill the freshly planted annuals and sprouting vegetables? Will I have to start again?

During periods of extended drought, I gaze wistfully out the window at the brown lawn and listen to every weather forecast, hoping for rain. Our soil is so sandy that we need frequent downpours to perk up the flowerbeds and keep the lawn green. I can water the beds with the hose, but not the lawn, unless I want to risk emptying the well.

Sometimes we face the opposite problem. The spring comes in late and rainy. The summer continues cold and wet. Whatever grows is spindly and watery. Vegetables lack taste. Flying, crawling, burrowing, munching insects throng the garden. We hanker for sunshine and dry days, but slip into autumn mouldy and miserable.

Dependence on the weather is dependence on God. Sunshine and rain are gifts of God's common grace—distinct from salvation, a gift of special grace. 'He causes his sun to rise on the evil and the good, and sends rain on the righteous and the unrighteous' (Matthew 5:45). As King Ahab discovered from Elijah, God can withhold the rain at any time. In Ahab's case, it was to punish Israel for its idolatry: 'it did not rain on the land for three and a half years' (James 5:17, referring to 1 Kings 18).

We may feel proud of a border full of bright flowers or a productive vegetable patch. But too often we fail to take note of how dependent we are on God's benevolence. If there were no sunshine and no water, we would have no garden.

We make the same mistake in the spiritual realm. If God had not sent his

Son to die for our sins and his Spirit to regenerate our sinful, selfish hearts, we would have no salvation. We would be eternally lost; 'when the kindness and love of God our Saviour appeared, he saved us, not because of righteous things we had done, but because of his mercy ... so that, having been justified by his grace, we might become heirs' (Titus 3:4–5,7).

We cannot rely upon our own works to save us, no matter how commendable they seem; we must put our faith in the work of Christ. It is God who arouses us to faith and plants new life in our dry and barren hearts. From beginning to end, salvation depends upon God's free grace: 'For it is by grace you have been saved, through faith—and this not from yourselves, it is the gift of God' (Ephesians 2:8).

Admittedly, there is a distinction between the faith that leads to salvation and trusting God for rain. The first requires us to make a choice. The latter usually happens whether we trust God or not. God sends his rain even on atheists! Nevertheless, like the wise gardener who recognizes God by placing his faith in God's sunshine and rain, the growing Christian continues to trust God for the day-to-day provision of sanctifying grace. As Jesus said, 'I am the vine; you are the branches ... apart from me you can do nothing' (John 15:5). Without ongoing faith in God's transforming grace, we cannot grow in our Christian lives.

While good works play no part in moving God to save us, genuine faith moves us to do good works. Faith that does not motivate us to adopt a disciplined approach to Christian living is a chimera. (A disciplined approach includes a consistent devotional life, participation in congregational celebration and expressing our gifts through service.)

Like the counterfeit Christian, the naive gardener who claims to trust God for a good crop but neither plants nor weeds the flower beds is not exercising faith but presumption. Christ warned us, 'Not everyone who says to me, "Lord, Lord," shall enter the kingdom of heaven, but he who does the will of my Father in heaven ... by their fruits you will know them' (Matthew 7:21,20).

Like gardeners, we thank God for good soil and believe that good things will happen. We trust that God will germinate the seeds, water our plants and energize their growth. And all summer, we work hard to cultivate the soil, root out the weeds and fertilize the garden.

Prayer
Father, I rejoice in the free gifts you give—not only sunshine and rain, but also salvation through Christ in spite of unspeakable sins. From beginning to end, your grace is amazing. Not only do you save me from the penalty of sin, but you also pour out your grace daily to deliver me from sin's pollution. Help me, through the Spirit, to root out evil thoughts and damaging habits, that you may produce good fruit in me. Amen.

Crows in convention

Bible reading
Acts 2:36–47

I was out for a walk one day down our country road when loud cawing attracted my attention to a tree across a distant field. A convention of crows blackened the tree. Glancing around, I spotted crows flying towards this congregation from every point of the compass. Strange! Was it curiosity that brought them winging their way from distant corners of the township? Or was it news of carrion to devour? Not speaking crow-talk, I couldn't tell, but it did remind me of the importance of gathering together with other Christians.

Crows are not solitary creatures; they forage in small flocks. Many birds and animals pass their lives in the company of others of their species: gaggles of geese; coveys of quail; herds of deer; packs of wolves.

Earth's gregarious creatures teach us many lessons, among them the importance of togetherness. The siren song of open fields and vast forests may make us enamoured with the wonder of solitude, but we need fellowship too.

In our noisy, crowded world, solitude is a treasure. We would all be much better off if we wrote 'No trespassing' over the special blocks of time when we seek God alone. But if we don't balance solitude with companionship, we run the risk of becoming eccentric, self-centred and antisocial.

With Mary Helen never far from my side, I'm fortunate to be seldom completely alone. We are often so contented with each other and our little corner in the country that we don't miss the crowded malls and busy streets of the city we left behind. Without care, we might even find excuses to stay home from church services. After all, gasoline is so expensive!

Taking that route would be extremely harmful. The early church 'devoted themselves to the apostles' teaching and to the fellowship, to the breaking of bread and to prayer ... All the believers were together ... Every day they continued to meet together in the temple courts. They broke bread in their homes and ate together with glad and sincere hearts' (Acts 2:42,44,46). The time would come when they would be scattered, but, even when hounded from place to place, they sought one another out. The strength they gained from togetherness enabled them to withstand persecution and thrive even while the society around them decayed.

Alone, we struggle against impossible odds to extend the kingdom. Alone, our potential is often unrealized or blunted. Alone, we are one-sided, unbalanced—caricatures of what we can be together. But in the context of a church fellowship, our gifts flower and the body of Christ is built up.

Following a solitary path through life creates distortions of viewpoint and character. By contrast, 'As iron sharpens iron, so one man sharpens another' (Proverbs 27:17). What is true of two people is doubly true of groups of people joined by their allegiance to Jesus Christ.

Alone, we are easy targets; twigs easily bent; susceptible to temptation, to whispers, to wild schemes, to treasuring an exalted opinion of ourselves. Therefore, 'Let us not give up meeting together, as some are in the habit of doing, but let us encourage one another—and all the more as you see the Day approaching' (Hebrews 10:25). Clearly, the writer to the Hebrews faced the same challenge in his day as we do in ours—of convincing people about the fundamental importance of regular Christian assembly. Too many in our day claim, 'We worship God quite well, thank you, on the golf course, in front of a TV set or while walking on the beach.'

Even when other Christians disappoint us—and they do—it is dangerous to conclude that we would be better off doing our own thing. Instead of complaining about our local church, we should give thanks for the opportunity to share our joys and sorrows with others whom Christ has called out of darkness. We need fellowship: the comforting, edifying, encouraging, challenging, worshipping company of others. (Don't misunderstand me here: many of our churches could use a healthy dose of self-criticism leading to genuine renewal. A vibrant church is always undergoing spiritual renovation.)

Some of us seem to be born with an independent streak. In weak moments, I dream of settling down in a log cabin in a lonely Rocky Mountain valley. Then I wake up to reality, to moods that can only be driven off by the exuberance or encouragement of others. I could list dozens of times when gloom or discouragement, even despair, has been banished by forcing myself to go to a prayer meeting, worship service or Bible study. Often the very act of sitting down with other believers raises the spirit. If crows instinctively band together, shouldn't we gather regularly with other believers to join our voices in worship and prayer?

Prayer

Heavenly Father, listen to my prayer as I bow in supplication and praise. Help me to treasure these times of quietness. But Lord, you know my temperament. Assist me to balance solitude with fellowship. You know, Master, that our church is far from perfect and I have many foibles. Move me to overlook the very human frailties of others, to celebrate the real evidences of your Spirit at work. Please help me not to forget that we are all spiritual beggars seeking bread. Speak to me through your servant's preaching. Unite my heart with others in worship. Guide me to join others in prayer. Use my gifts to serve the church. May I be an encouragement, a comfort, a blessing to others. Lord, I thank you for the times when you meet me in solitude, and the many times you come close in the midst of the church family! Amen.

july

Trash on the trail

Bible reading
Philippians 4:4–9

Mary Helen frowned when she came in from a walk one day. She described the first part of her walk in rather lyrical terms: 'After the rain, everything looked and smelled fresh and vibrant. Birds chattered and sang to me as I walked along. Happiness filled my heart. I felt so thankful for my Father's goodness. Then I saw it!

'It immediately scattered my cheerful thoughts. Garbage by the side of the road! Someone had tossed out a whole bag of containers from a fast-food outlet. A little further along, I saw more garbage. How could anyone be so thoughtless? What kind of a person can't wait until they find a trash container to get rid of their rubbish?

'My mood had suddenly shifted. But, when I realized that I was letting garbage ruin my walk, I gave myself a good shake. This is so much like life. I sometimes get so distracted by what is ugly in life that I fail to celebrate what is beautiful.'

The lesson Mary Helen drew from trash reminds us all to focus more on the positive than on the negative.

We cannot deny that life has no shortage of garbage moments: someone cuts us up in traffic or we receive a scary diagnosis. I'm sure God does not expect us to ignore trash or sail through difficult times with nary a tear. However, Mary Helen was right in refusing to let garbage distract her from enjoying a beautiful day. I have to admit that she's much better at doing that than I am.

I'm reminded of the amazing message of Philippians. Although the author, the apostle Paul, was in Roman chains facing possible death, he wrote a 'joy epistle'. Six times he talked about joy. 'I always pray with joy because of your partnership in the gospel' (Philippians 1:4–5). Nine times he mentioned rejoicing. 'Rejoice in the Lord always. I will say it again: Rejoice!' (4:4).

In part, Paul's optimism can be traced to his determination to direct his mind away from thoughts of garbage. Reflecting this mindset, he exhorted the Philippians in these immortal words: 'whatever is true, whatever is noble, whatever is right, whatever is pure, whatever is lovely, whatever is admirable—if anything is excellent or praiseworthy—think about such things' (4:8). Paul does not ignore problems, persecution or pain, but he does inject a hopeful outlook in all his writings. If he were walking down our road, he might see the trash but choose to focus more on the wildflowers.

Some of us are pessimists. We allow a distant cloud to spoil our enjoyment of sunshine. We gloss over the flowers to focus on the weeds. We miss the rainbow in the rainstorm. The weather is either too hot, too cold, too wet or too dry. We find the preacher either used too many illustrations or not enough. I blush to admit to being a member of Pessimists Anonymous—I'm still taking the cure.

In Paul's case, his hopeful outlook can be traced to his God-centred view of life. He rejoiced that, whatever the devil might do in Philippi, he could not thwart God's grace. 'I always pray with joy … being confident of this, that he who began a good work in you will carry it on to completion until the day of Christ Jesus' (1:4,6). Bad things will happen to us, but nothing will stop God from completing his gracious work in our midst.

Paul realized that his imprisonment furthered God's purposes: 'What has happened to me has really served to advance the gospel … [It is] clear throughout the whole palace guard and to everyone else that I am in chains for Christ' (1:12–13). What chance has discouragement to gain a foothold if we embrace such a vision?

And yet, Paul is not naively optimistic. He made these statements without ignoring the garbage around him in Rome and in the Philippian church. He wrote that some even 'preach Christ out of envy and rivalry … from false motives' (1:15,18). He reminded them that they lived 'in a crooked and depraved generation' (2:15). Many of his co-workers, with the exception of Timothy and Epaphroditus, were looking out for their own interests and not those of Jesus Christ (2:19–30). They were in danger of being enslaved by legalistic teachers (3:2–3,18–19). Disunity was also a hazard (4:2–3).

These concerns, added to the severity of Paul's circumstances, might have led Paul to write a very pessimistic epistle. Yet he didn't. He had such a high view of the purpose of Christ, and of the overwhelming value of being forgiven and declared righteous in Christ, that everything else seemed insignificant:

I consider everything a loss compared to the surpassing greatness of knowing Christ Jesus my Lord ... the righteousness that comes from God and is by faith ... I press on to take hold of that for which Christ Jesus took hold of me ... Forgetting what is behind and straining towards what is ahead, I press on towards the goal to win the prize for which God has called me heavenwards in Christ Jesus (3:7–9,12–14).

As we emulate Paul's hopeful, positive outlook, we too will be enabled to look beyond this world's troubles and trash to recognize the onward march of God's kingdom.

Prayer

Father, continue to overcome my bent towards pessimism. Help me not to miss the blessings you scatter along my pathway. Train me to think about good, beautiful and praiseworthy things and not to focus on garbage. Give me a heavenly perspective that enables me to see beyond problems to recognize your providence. Help me to value what Christ values. For yours is the kingdom and the power and the glory for ever. Amen.

The growth imperative

Bible reading

Colossians 1:3–14

It was one of those ideal summers: warm weather with rain at regular intervals. The grass stayed green throughout August. Flowers bloomed through September. The tomato harvest was enough for an extended family of Italians. The beans kept right on producing all summer.

The year of dramatic growth was also the year of creepy crawlies. I had ants, slugs, caterpillars and earwigs, plus all kinds of unknown insects, all bent on eating their way through every plant in sight.

Spiritual growth, like growth in my garden, is always contested. But whatever the setbacks, a person with genuine faith in Christ will show evidence of some measure of growth. Paul thanked God for the Thessalonians 'because your faith is growing more and more, and the love every one of you has for each other is increasing. Therefore, among God's churches we boast about your perseverance and faith in all the persecutions and trials you are enduring' (2 Thessalonians 1:3–4).

Paul commended the Colossians for their growth in hope, faith and love: 'We have heard of your faith in Christ Jesus and of the love you have for all the saints—the faith and love that spring from the hope that is stored up for you in heaven' (Colossians 1:4–5).

Peter wrote, 'But grow in the grace and knowledge of our Lord and Saviour Jesus Christ' (2 Peter 3:18). The maturing Christian shows a developing knowledge of Christ. Such knowledge fosters an increasing celebration of grace—God's undeserved favour. This, in turn, strengthens the believer's appreciation of all the gifts Christ gives us in salvation, including forgiveness, justification and sanctification.

Spiritual development can be viewed from many perspectives: increase in faith, hope and love; more Christlikeness; growth in manifestation of the fruits of the Spirit; an intensifying prayer life; increasing understanding of the Bible and more application to life; growth in worship and thanksgiving.

Spiritual progress is so crucial that I need frequently to ask myself, 'Am I changing for the better?' Lack of growth may signal either lack of a genuine conversion experience or some hindrance to growth.

We should not become too easily discouraged. Every garden situation brings its challenges and every maturing Christian faces new temptations. The devil is determined to hinder our growth. He may discourage us or puff us up with pride. He may use worry about the future or fear of illness. He may tempt us to embrace worldly pursuits and activities or lead us into a self-righteous asceticism. He sometimes provokes us through colleagues at work, a neighbour where we live or a pastor at church. He may lead us into believing gossip or accepting heretical ideas. His weapons are manifold.

Satan, however, cannot withstand the power of the gospel. Wherever people respond positively to its message, growth is assured. Paul writes of the Colossians, 'All over the world this gospel is bearing fruit and growing, just as it has been doing among you since the day you heard it and understood God's grace in all its truth' (Colossians 1:6).

The only way to keep a garden growing is to remember the basics: cultivate, water, weed, fertilize and watch out for bugs and blight. In the same way, we withstand the attacks of the evil one by never straying from the gospel basics. We rejoice that the same grace that saved us from our sins keeps us in God's love. We may stumble and fall, but Christ is always there to forgive us and cleanse us from all unrighteousness. We trust in the indwelling Holy Spirit, who is infinitely greater than the devil. We overcome the devil through the blood of the covenant.

Every day, I wander through my garden, checking on its growth. Similarly, we need to give daily attention to our spiritual condition. Instituting a daily time for Bible reading and prayer helps immensely. So does making a habit of joining other Christians for teaching and worship every week. Being involved in some kind of ministry keeps us sharp. Spiritual disciplines such as these are important, but let's make sure we don't depend on anything but grace to keep us growing. The most disciplined of spiritual gymnastics cannot do what God does in answer to prayer.

Of course, growth takes time. Sometimes we get impatient with ourselves or others when we don't perceive much change. It could be that we need the perspective of time.

A few weeks before writing this, Mary Helen and I visited a church where we had served in the past. Two of the young couples whose weddings I had conducted were leaders in the church. Several women from the youth group now comprised the worship team. The kid with all the questions was now an elder!

We all draw strength and encouragement from seeing the growth of other Christians. That's probably why reading a good biography is so beneficial. And, if the story is an honest account, we'll see that growth seldom occurs in an uninterrupted upward spiral. All of us go through periods of spiritual drought. But we can be confident with Paul that 'he who began a good work in you will carry it on to completion until the day of Christ Jesus' (Philippians 1:6). The devil cannot stop the growth of a truly converted soul.

Prayer
Father, help me to grow in celebration of your grace. Lord Jesus Christ, help me to know you better and to become more like you. Such a long way to go! The demands of my fallen nature are so subtle. Teach me to recognize and reject them more forcefully. Show me how to love others more, to trust you more, to be more hopeful. Holy Spirit, develop within me the necessary fruits of Christian character. Keep me growing. Amen.

Of butterflies
and noxious plants

Bible reading
Genesis 1:27–31

A yearly warning to get rid of noxious weeds on our property arrives with our municipal tax bill. An unspecified fine is threatened. But what are noxious weeds? I know from experience that poison ivy is a menace. I've had its blisters pop up too often to ignore it. And ragweed seems to cause the misery of hay fever. But what about milkweed?

As children, the milk that oozed from a broken milkweed stem fascinated us. And we'd often decorate the dried pods for Christmas. Otherwise, the plant seems useless—a noxious weed. However, researchers have discovered that the milkweed leaf is the only food that monarch caterpillars eat. Since the milkweed is poisonous to most predators, it keeps the spectacularly coloured monarch butterflies safe. What if we had obliterated all the milkweed in Ontario? No more monarchs!

The absence of these magnificent butterflies wouldn't cause a ripple in the financial markets. But thousands in North America would be saddened. Every year, I look forward to seeing them flit around my garden.

Is the beauty of the monarchs and the pleasure they bring enough to agitate for the survival of milkweed? Or must something be useful to be conserved?

Beauty or utility? How is the Christian to approach questions of conservation like these? In Genesis 1 we read about what has been called the cultural mandate: 'Be fruitful and increase in number; fill the earth and subdue it. Rule over the fish of the sea and the birds of the air and over every living creature that moves on the ground' (v. 28). Chapter 2 describes a garden where God placed Adam 'to work it and take care of it' (v. 15).

Clearly, God gives mankind permission to use the earth and its resources for human benefit. But don't the words 'subdue' and 'rule over' sound ominous? Could this command include permission to rape and pillage the earth? To burn its rain forests? To deplete the seas of fish? To hunt bears for their body parts? To fill our oceans with PCBs? To confine farm animals to narrow pens in vast factories that pollute the groundwater for miles around? No, a thousand times, no!

God calls us to treasure and care for the earth, including all its resources—animal, vegetable and mineral. Eventually, he will judge us for our stewardship, including the legacy we leave. We have no right to disrupt the earth's fragile balance for short-term gain. We have no right to allow the extinction of a species just because it seems to serve no useful purpose.

Who but God, the Creator of all, can really understand what some call 'the balance of nature'? God created a world of living things interconnected by their dependence on one another. At the very beginning, God said, ' ... to all the beasts of the earth and all the birds of the air and the creatures that move on the ground—everything that has the breath of life in it—I give every green plant for food' (Genesis 1:30). Biodiversity and ecological balance are creation concepts.

Failure to conserve the unique habitats of the earth will harm mankind. Not only will the destruction of the rainforest deplete earth's store of oxygen, but it will also diminish the gene pool. Perhaps the cure for malaria, cancer or Alzheimer's disease is out there somewhere, waiting to be discovered.

Even if no use is found within our lifetimes for obscure species, we still have a responsibility to preserve their existence because God declared them to be 'good' (see Genesis 1:10–12,20–21,24–25). Surely we don't want to be found guilty of destroying what God has declared 'good'! We'll frequently be unable to point out any practical usefulness for a plant or creature. Perhaps some things exist only because God delights in creating complexity and beauty. Preserving living things that project the artistry of the Creator must be a Christian duty.

To return to the monarch butterfly, who can deny that God declared it to be 'good'? Who can deny that God has given it the milkweed for food? Even so, monarchs remained a mystery until recent times.

Before 1975, it was not known that the monarch butterflies of eastern

North America migrated. It was assumed that they died out and a new flock was born in the spring. Curious, Fred Urquhart used tiny tags to trace their migration to the Mexican border. Then a young couple discovered their winter habitat two miles high in the Michoacan Mountains of Mexico. What a sight met their eyes: tens of millions of butterflies thronging groves of oyamel trees! They had migrated from as far as James Bay, 1,800 miles away.

When logging threatened to destroy the groves, an international effort led to the creation of a Mexican butterfly sanctuary 216 square miles in size. The future looks promising for the monarch butterfly. Is God pleased? I believe so.

Followers of Christ rightly give priority to the Great Commission— rescuing lost men and women from hell. But too often we neglect the cultural commission which calls us to be stewards of the earth.

Prayer

Lord, you created this astonishing world for our benefit and your glory. We reap enormous riches from land and sea. As if this were not enough, you have surrounded us with the incredible beauty of your handiwork. Yet often we have not glorified you as Creator. We have not fulfilled our stewardship well. Our seas are becoming depleted; our water and air polluted. Our descendants are threatened.

Heavenly Father, increase awareness among Christians of this issue. Lord, raise up from the Christian church a mighty army of men and women committed to conservation and the ecological health of the planet. Help me to do my part where I live. In Jesus' name. Amen.

Rain that hardens

Bible reading
Hebrews 5:11–6:12

'Summertime, an' the livin' is easy.' Ah, lazy, warm days. The season to wander the countryside. Time to lounge on the veranda and gaze in pride at our flower beds and vegetable garden. But wait! All is not well. The plants look a little stunted. Thistles threaten the beans.

I love our garden, but not always the work involved. So sometimes I just take it easy. I let nature take its course—especially when we're away for a week or rain frees me from my watering duties. Unfortunately, rain also signals 'Go' to all kinds of weeds. How is it that the plants we don't want grow twice as fast as those we desire?

With a sigh, I abandon my iced tea and pick up my trowel. Obviously, the beds need weeding and cultivating. Although nothing stops weeds, rain compacts the ground and restricts the growth of everything else. If I don't loosen the soil, it will become as hard as concrete—unless I spend a fortune on organic soil conditioners. Since I'm not Bill Gates, I get down on my knees and break up the soil.

Farmers know that a fruitful harvest cannot occur unless they first break up hard soil to make it workable. The prophet Hosea used this image to illustrate his hearers' need to soften their hearts through repentance: 'Break up your unploughed ground; for it is time to seek the LORD' (Hosea 10:12). Hosea was warning the people of Israel that they would never harvest the 'fruit of [God's] unfailing love' unless they allowed their hard hearts to be ploughed by a rigorous self-examination.

The writer of Hebrews used a similar metaphor to expose the stunted nature of his readers' faith: 'Land that drinks in the rain often falling on it and that produces a crop useful to those for whom it is farmed receives the blessing of God. But land that produces thorns and thistles is worthless … In the end it will be burned' (Hebrews 6:7–8).

Too much rain without cultivation encourages the thorns and thistles that stifle fruitful plants. The writer of Hebrews compares the application of truth to life with the weeding and cultivation that produce a fruitful crop. When we apply what we hear, our hearts remain soft and teachable. Unfortunately, the writer found his readers lazy about application: 'you are slow to learn ... you need someone to teach you the elementary truths of God's word all over again. You need milk, not solid food!' (5:11–12). Stuck in spiritual infancy, these Hebrew Christians couldn't digest the strong teaching needed for maturing in Christ. They listened again and again to simple truths but never trained 'themselves to distinguish good from evil' (5:14). As a result, they made no progress, and this lack of application moved the writer to question the reality of their faith.

Although the rain of the gospel had fallen on the Hebrews abundantly, it yielded no fruit. In this metaphor, they were fields that drank in the water of the Word but remained barren.

James expressed the same concern: 'Do not merely listen to the word, and so deceive yourselves. Do what it says. Anyone who listens to the word but does not do what it says is like a man who looks at his face in a mirror and, after looking at himself, goes away and immediately forgets what he looks like' (James 1:22–24).

Fortunately, in the case of the Hebrews, the author was 'confident of better things' in them (Hebrews 6:9). Does God find us teachable? Do we obey his commands? Do we listen to his Word and make specific practical applications? From the messages we hear on Sundays, do we take home lessons that we can incorporate into our lifestyles?

Do we take steps to reach out to our neighbours after a message on evangelism? After a devotional study on encouragement, do we determine to write one note a week to friends? On Monday morning, do we begin to set aside more time in our devotions for worship? On Monday night, do we watch less TV and take up that uplifting book we started months ago?

Prayer

Father, soften my heart. Make me teachable. Keep me from ever taking your Word for granted. Continue to thrill me with your love and grace. Intrigue me with your truth. Give me a listening heart open to the whispers of your will. Help me to walk in obedience to your desires. Amen.

august

The summer that wasn't

Bible reading
Jeremiah 1¹

I remember vividly the summer that wasn't. I would wake, hoping that a new day would bring sunshine and clear skies. Instead, there was another overcast day of intermittent rain. Even in early July, one of the statistically driest, hottest weeks of the Canadian summer was soggy and cool. The lawn was waterlogged; all the veggies late. The farmers bit their fingernails as they eyed hay that needed cutting and wheat that needed harvesting.

Paradoxically, long-range forecasts had predicted a warmer-than-usual summer. A Canadian forecaster admitted that they had been only thirty per cent right that year. He even confessed that a non-techie could probably do as well as this. American pundits carried the same lament. Yet today's meteorologists use the most sophisticated weather-predicting equipment ever assembled.

Without any equipment, biblical prophets score an accuracy rate of one hundred per cent. By contrast, if forecasters even score an unlikely high of ninety per cent, an unpredictable hurricane—part of the ten per cent they miss—can still wreak devastation. Of course, meteorologists have to rely on human calculations, whereas biblical prophets relied on the words of the sovereign Lord. We should not be surprised, then, that whatever God predicts comes to pass without fail.

Yet the accuracy of the Bible's prophecies is astonishing. The Koran, the Hindu Vedas and the Bhagavadgita do not contain prophecy. The same can be said of Buddha's sayings, those of Confucius and the Book of Mormon. Around thirty per cent of the Bible's content, however, contains prophecy—part of which is prediction, and part preaching.

Jesus' life and death followed an outline laid out in prophecy centuries before his birth. In the Gospels, a refrain draws our attention to this fact: 'All this took place to fulfil what the Lord had said through the prophet … "this is what the prophet has written" … and so was fulfilled what the Lord had said through the prophet' (see Matthew 1:22; 2:5,15,17; 3:3; etc.). The way in which Jesus' life fulfilled prophecy is nothing short of miraculous.

Consider several more obscure prophecies. John Blanchard writes, 'Around 920 BC, an unnamed prophet told Jeroboam, the first King of [divided] Israel, that his throne would one day be occupied by a king called Josiah, who would sweep away the widespread idolatry promoted by Jeroboam. This seemed nonsensical to the all-powerful Jeroboam but 300 years later Josiah [did just as predicted].'[2]

Take another example. Between 740 and 700 BC, Isaiah predicted a series of events including the fall of Jerusalem, the Babylonian captivity, the return of the exiles and the rebuilding of the temple under someone named Cyrus. Around 200 years later, these events transpired exactly as prophesied. Without divine inspiration, Isaiah could not have known the name of the future king of a kingdom (Persia) that was not even in existence during his lifetime.

Scores of other examples could be cited. To demonstrate the impossibility of prophetic fulfilment being the result of chance, Peter Stoner picked eleven prophecies. As explained in his book *Science Speaks*, he calculated that the probability of their fulfilment would be 1 in 8×10^{63}. John Blanchard explains what this would mean:

If we were to scoop together a pile of coins equal to 100 billion stars in each of two trillion galaxies in just one second, and then add to the pile at the same rate every second, day and night, for twenty-one years, we would be ready for the test. If we then asked a blindfolded friend to pick out one marked coin from this incomprehensibly massive pile, his chances of doing so would be one in 8×10^{63}, the same as the likelihood that [the prophets would have got things right by guesswork].[3]

I appreciate weather forecasters. They do the best they can with their equipment, but, when I want certainty about the future, I turn to the Bible. The future is in the hand of the Father. We need not fear the unknown. The trumpet will sound and the dead in Christ will arise. Jesus will return with all his saints. Every eye will see him. There will be a day of judgement and all evil will be overcome. Satan will be cast into the lake of fire. Tears will be wiped away. The kingdom will come. All this, and much more, we can know for sure.

Prayer
Eternal God, I read the prophets with amazement. Thank you for the astounding book you have given us, accurate in all it affirms—past, present and future. Although my understanding of all the details about the future is quite limited, I know I can trust you to work it out for your glory—perfectly. The future is in your hands. Amen!

Notes

1 Compare Isaiah 44:28 with Ezra 1:1–3; see also 2 Peter 1:12–21; Revelation 22.
2 **John Blanchard,** *Does God Believe In Atheists?* (Darlington: Evangelical Press, 2000), p. 409. Read Blanchard's short but excellent section on prophecy from pp. 407 to 410. For this specific prophecy, compare 1 Kings 13:1–2 with 2 Kings 21:25–22:2; 23:15–18.
3 Ibid., pp. 409–410.

Little bandits
and a big principle

Bible reading
Luke 6:27–38

The big day arrived, the day to pick the first ripe tomato! My mouth watered as I sauntered out to the tomato patch. Shock! All that remained of my prize tomato was a gnawed shell sitting in a row of crushed beet-tops. Bandito raccoon had struck again!

God displayed a sense of humour when he created raccoons with the robber's mask already in place. Most days, these little bandits don't make me smile. They repeatedly raid our heavy plastic composter, knocking the top off. A couple of times a year, they crush my flowers in an attempt to get at the birdseed in the bird feeder.

Come to think of it, our neighbourhood is full of little bandits. Rabbits munch my lettuce and Swiss chard. Mice get into everything. Squirrels sneak into the garage to gnaw the plastic top off my grass-seed container and scatter the hulls everywhere. I don't dare plant corn with raccoons and deer on the prowl.

The depredations of our animal bandits are fairly harmless. All we need to do is plant a bit extra. Anyway, they're so likeable: bunnies, raccoons, squirrels, chipmunks and deer. But they do remind me of a most unattractive human tendency.

Reflecting the animal inclination to take rather than give, raccoons give nothing back to their victims except muddy footprints. Agur, in the book of Proverbs, picks the leech as the ultimate exemplar of this attitude: 'The leech has two daughters. "Give! Give!" they cry' (Proverbs 30:15).

We don't have to cite statistics about dishonesty or bank robbery to establish that humans share this propensity. In *The Globe and Mail*, Ian Brown wrote about freeloaders who sponge off their friends and relatives. To understand his subject, Brown experimented by freeloading for a month off his brother. Tongue-in-cheek, he described people who set out to prove 'the popular theory of modern life that you have to take what you can while you can'.[1]

We could add to the list of freeloaders: people who will not travel unless they can stay in the home of an acquaintance; perpetual guests who are never hosts. Then there are those who borrow books and tools but never return them.

Perpetual victims also illustrate this principle—ever taking, never giving. The very laudable advances in social programmes in our Western democracies seem to have created a whole new class of 'victims' who expect governments to provide them with everything from the cradle to the grave. An attitude of entitlement has threatened the much-lampooned Protestant work ethic. On every hand we hear, 'Why doesn't the government do this, give this, take care of that?' Yet many refrain from participating in a census or voting in elections and, if possible, avoid paying taxes. (I am not denying the existence of those who need help. Genuinely needy people deserve compassion.)

Even conversation provides lots of examples of the take-instead-of-give syndrome. Good listeners are very rare. We often approach conversation with the goal of getting attention, getting our point across or telling our story instead of listening to what others have to say. Kind listening requires that we give people the gift of our sincere attention to what they are saying. That means setting aside our own agenda. Takers are common; givers, rare—even in conversation.

Sponging; freeloading; stealing; singing the artificial victim's lament; taking over conversations and never listening: all of these are symptoms of the fallen nature that Christ calls us to crucify and replace with a new desire to give rather than take: 'Give, and it will be given to you. A good measure, pressed down, shaken together and running over, will be poured into your lap. For with the measure you use, it will be measured to you' (Luke 6:38).

Paul reminded the Ephesian elders, 'the Lord Jesus himself said: "It is more blessed to give than to receive"' (Acts 20:35). An essential attribute of God himself is love. Love gives generously: 'For God so loved the world that he gave his one and only Son' (John 3:16). In his first epistle, John often reiterates, 'God is love. Whoever lives in love lives in God, and God in him.'

In other words, the infallible mark that distinguishes a child of God from a child of the devil is love for others. Practically speaking, this means that God transforms his children from takers into givers.

Time for confession: this tendency even rears its ugly head in the worship service—when I catch myself evaluating a service in terms of what I got out of it. Were the people friendly to me? Did I like the music? Was the preaching interesting or boring? Instead, I should ask myself, 'Was I a blessing to someone at church today? Was my response to God and his Word a blessing to him?'

Prayer

Lord, I can't blame the animals for doing what comes naturally. But I am no longer a slave to my fallen human nature as they are to theirs. No, I've been born again by your Spirit! Help me to put to death the old tendency selfishly to take. Help me to put on the new nature, created to love and give. Today—indeed, every day—make me a blessing to others and to you. Amen.

Notes

1 **Ian Brown,** 'Freeloading: It Runs in the Family', *The Globe and Mail*, 19 August 2006, p. F3.

Savouring summer

Bible reading

Psalm 34

Summer calls us to indulge in a cornucopia of wonderful tastes. Forget haute cuisine; I'd rather sample sun-kissed garden produce any day: local strawberries; home-grown lettuce; new potatoes; peas and beans picked in the morning and smothered in butter in the evening; tender young cucumbers; local corn, whose kernels, when tested, squirt milk in your eye; and especially the taste of sun-ripened local tomatoes—a flavour to carry with us through the cold days of winter.

I can almost taste a fresh, home-grown tomato as I write: thick slices on a hunk of sourdough bread. Whew, I wish the sun would hurry them to our table! Then we could forget about all those gassed clones shipped from Florida or Mexico, or those hothouse tomatoes trying desperately to conjure up some of the flavour of a sun-drenched tomato from a local garden.

Taste is another of God's astonishing gifts of grace. David used taste as a metaphor to illustrate the apex of human experiences: 'Taste and see that the LORD is good; blessed is the man who takes refuge in him' (Psalm 34:8).

David wrote about God's goodness during a desperate time. He was fleeing for his life from King Saul's murderous jealousy. He and his men had taken refuge with Saul's enemy, the king of Gath. Alarmed, Gath's advisors warned that David represented a greater threat than Saul. To blunt this perception, David first pretended madness, then escaped further into the wilderness.

In spite of the danger of betrayal and death, David penned an amazing psalm of praise:

I will extol the LORD at all times …
I sought the LORD and he answered me;
   he delivered me from all my fears …
This poor man called, and the LORD heard him;

he saved him out of all his troubles.
The angel of the LORD encamps around those who fear him,
    and he delivers them.
Taste and see that the LORD is good (Psalm 34:1,4,6–8).

David's psalm illustrates the experience of many saints who have endured great suffering. People come to know God deeply when they cry out to him: in trials, in persecutions, in pain, in sadness, in grief, in danger, in poverty. When fear grips our hearts and we desperately call out to God, he often gives a life-changing sense of his presence. 'The LORD is close to the brokenhearted and saves those who are crushed in spirit' (v. 18). Without this element of desperation and helplessness, we often cruise through life, trusting in our own abilities to solve problems. We may know about God, but we don't savour his goodness.

Like many people, I had picky eating habits as a child. I didn't like pickles or onions; now I love them both. I didn't like shrimp; today, it's one of my favourites. I certainly didn't like spicy foods; then we lived for years in Pakistan, where everything was cooked with garlic, onions, chilli peppers and turmeric. Now, we savour these flavours.

What happened to change my taste in foods? I got dumped into situations where I had to try different dishes. Boarding meals at college; dinners at friends' homes; immersion in the Pakistani culture: I quickly learned that, if I didn't want to starve, I needed to try new foods. Tasting new foods led to the revelation: 'Hey, that really tastes good!'

Sadly, vast numbers of people have poor spiritual taste buds. Some see evil in the world and blame God; others just ignore him. Some deny his existence; others perceive him to be the cause of the bad things that happen to them. None of these have really tasted God's goodness. They know nothing about God because God is beyond their experience.

Those who cry out to God in their extremity experience his goodness: 'I sought the LORD, and he answered me … This poor man called, and the LORD heard him; he saved him out of all his troubles.' Those who cry out, those who seek, 'taste and see that the LORD is good'.

Every believer knows something of God's goodness. How good is God, the Father, who loved us enough to send his son! How good is God, the

Son, who died while bearing our sins! How good is God, the Spirit, who stoops to dwell within our tarnished hearts!

Without some sense of God's goodness, Christian growth is impossible. Imagine having no taste for food: no delight in fresh produce or—for many of us—a perfectly grilled T-bone steak. These remembered tastes call us back for more. Pointing to the growth of infants, Peter writes, 'Like newborn babies, crave pure spiritual milk, so that by it you may grow up in your salvation.' He goes on to point out that this craving comes to those who 'have tasted that the Lord is good' (1 Peter 2:2–3).

The memory of the first ripe tomatoes fills me with longing. And the memory of past experiences of God's goodness makes me hungry for more of his presence. Certainly, an explosion of taste sensations will follow us into eternity as God reveals more and more of his glory and grace.

Prayer
Father, I have tasted your goodness. One glance at the cross confronts me with your love. Another glance down through the years reminds me that 'goodness and love' have followed me 'all the days of my life' [Psalm 23:6]. Sometimes, your goodness shone in privation; sometimes, in days of sunshine and success; sometimes, in pain; sometimes, in utter inadequacy and fear. Lord, please don't let my hunger and thirst for your presence fade into a distant memory. Amen.

Farmer ants

Bible reading
Philippians 2:1–11

One year, the tender new leaves on every branch of my cherry tree became stunted and curled. Curious, and rather annoyed, I grasped one of the branches and uncurled the leaves. Ants ran everywhere. One ran up my arm and gave me a sharp nip.

Closer inspection revealed that the ants were guarding a herd of aphids sucking sap from the tender veins of the leaves. Intrigued, I searched on the Internet for information and discovered that honeypot ants milk aphids for their honeydew secretions. Many ant species aggressively protect their aphids and move them from danger. Some species even carry their aphids to underground burrows during the winter months.

Fascinated, I couldn't bring myself to spray the tree. Instead, every day I unfurled the leaves to check on my cowboy ants. Boy, did they get riled! Then, a week or so later, they disappeared. Gone to some more peaceful pasture?

The aphids derived some benefit from the ants in terms of protection and placement. The ants, however, benefited most. Their domination of their aphid servants reminds me of two very unattractive human traits— manipulation and control.

Sophisticated consumers readily recognize manipulation in advertising. Do I really want to buy a gas-guzzling SUV just to enhance my persona? Can I live without the latest triple-size bacon-mushroom-melt-burger? Would I be wise to buy a new living-room suite at nothing down, no interest and no payments for two years?

What we recognize in advertisers we may overlook in ourselves. Society frowns on ordering people around. Instead, we may use guilt to manipulate others even though it infringes on their personal freedom. A boss: 'It's your decision, of course, but if we don't get this report done by Monday, we'll lose the contract.' An elderly parent: 'You never visit any more. Well, I won't be around much longer.' An adult son or daughter: 'I didn't ask to be born. The least you can do is loan me the money.'

Manipulative people even use religion to powerful effect. Suggestions that committed Christians do this or that are used to urge people to volunteer. Ministers sometimes misinterpret a biblical passage to get across their own agenda. Another favourite trick is to suggest that failure to attend every scheduled church meeting shows a lack of commitment. Sadly, some pastors carry manipulation and control to such a level that they become what Professor Earl Radmacher calls 'petty, Protestant, parochial popes'.

Evangelists and healers may orchestrate the atmosphere in their meetings to manipulate people's emotions. Rare is the evangelist who warns potential converts of the trials and persecution ahead. Instead, most emphasize the benefits of salvation: joy, peace, satisfaction, significance and eternal security.

A few relief agencies employ manipulation to garner support: 'Can you look at this child and deny it the price of a cup of coffee a day?'

Not content with subtlety, some control others more directly. Parents, employers, politicians, husbands, wives, bullies in the schoolyard, gang leaders and police are all tempted to abuse their positions. The desire to control others is as addictive as alcohol, and as destructive. This desire often lies behind rape and domestic abuse.

Jesus turns all these patterns on their head:

You know that the rulers of the Gentiles lord it over them, and their high officials exercise authority over them. Not so with you. Instead, whoever wants to become great among you must be your servant, and whoever wants to be first must be your slave—just as the Son of Man did not come to be served, but to serve, and to give his life as a ransom for many (Matthew 20:25–28).

Christ repudiates anything that smacks of coercion, manipulation, force or control. Christian leadership is gentle: 'A bruised reed [like sorrowful Peter] he will not break, and a smouldering wick [like Thomas with his flickering faith] he will not snuff out' (Matthew 12:20). We're astounded by Jesus' tender treatment of the woman with the issue of blood, the hungry throngs, hated tax collectors, an adulterous woman and even his betrayer, Judas.

Listen to his instructions through Paul, his apostle:

Do nothing out of selfish ambition or vain conceit, but in humility consider others better than yourselves. Each of you should look not only to your own interests, but also to the interests of others.

Your attitude should be the same as that of Christ Jesus:

Who, being in very nature God,

did not consider equality with God something to be grasped [held onto],

but made himself nothing,

taking the very nature of a servant,

being made in human likeness ...

he humbled himself and became obedient to death

(Philippians 2:3–8).

These words reflect the Beatitudes, where Christ taught us that citizens of his kingdom exhibit humility, meekness, mercy, peacefulness, purity of heart and stamina in the face of persecution (see Matthew 5:3–12). As these qualities infuse our personalities they overcome our desires to control others. In their place, the Spirit creates a longing to serve.

While God has a right to expect us to obey his commandments, he does not force us into conformity. Certainly, no human leader has the right to do what God does not do. Since we have one Lord, let us then refuse to manipulate or be manipulated.

Prayer

Father, deliver me from any desire to manipulate or control others. It's so easy to let a desire to have my own way overwhelm my restraint. I naturally think up strategies to convince others of the rightness of my desires. It's so unnatural for me to pray instead of demand, serve instead of expecting to be served.

Help me to be strong in faith but gentle in relationships. Amen.

Birdsong

Bible reading
Psalm 65

Birdsong fills the air. Robins serenade the rising sun. A cardinal whistles its distinctive tune. Goldfinches warble. The melodic notes of song sparrows reverberate from tree to tree. Mourning doves coo. Chickadees chatter. Somewhere down the slope near the stream, a bass drum sounds—a ruffled grouse strutting his stuff. Not to be outdone, a woodpecker picks up the tune on a hollow tree. The echoes reverberate throughout the valley.

I envy our feathered friends their musical prowess. Ever since I was around ten years old, when I failed an audition for a part in a Stephen Foster musical, I've avoided singing in public. Tough, when one is a pastor expected to lead in congregational singing! I had to make it very clear, wherever I served, that singing was not one of my abilities. When seated in a congregation, I keep my voice low enough so that neighbouring worshippers aren't distracted by my off-key renditions. When I wax too loud, Mary Helen gives me a jab.

The fact that I'm musically challenged doesn't mean I don't love music; I often tune in to the local classical station or play CDs while I work. Music is one of God's greatest gifts. It captures our moods. It encourages our hearts. It instructs our minds. It lifts us from darkness into light. Through music, we rise on the wings of angels to join the throngs around the throne.

With such a wonderful God to celebrate, it's no wonder that God's children love to sing. From the songbook of the Old Testament to Handel's *Messiah*; from Isaac Watts and Charles Wesley to the explosion of contemporary music in our day—whatever you may think about today's bards—believers sing on their way to heaven.

Moses and Deborah celebrated deliverance with song. David sang everywhere: in the mountains with his flock of sheep, deep in a cave when hunted by his enemies, on the road to Zion while bringing up the ark, and especially in the temple. His son, Solomon, composed 1,005 songs, including the sweet 'Song of Songs'. Even one of Job's supposed comforters got it right when he spoke of God giving songs in the night. Paul and Silas sang in prison. In the Bible's climactic vision of future glory we see the hosts of heaven singing the song of Moses and the new song of the Lamb (Deuteronomy 32; Judges 5; 1 Kings 4:30–32; Job 35:10; Acts 16:25; Ephesians 5:19; Revelation 5:9; 14:3; 15:3).

Around the earth, churches emulate the Bible's songsters. Sadly, embarrassment at my poor singing voice restricts how much I sing around the house—I don't want to assail Mary Helen's ears. Perhaps that's why too often I forget to leaf through the hymnbook. What a treasure! Like the songbirds, it encourages us to awaken the day with song:

When morning gilds the skies,
My heart awaking cries,
May Jesus Christ be praised.[1]

In the morning, before our necessary duties intervene, and then as the day ends, we would be wise to emulate the sweet psalmist of Israel who wrote, 'where morning dawns and evening fades you call forth songs of joy' (Psalm 65:8).

Joyful, joyful, we adore thee
God of glory, Lord of love;
Hearts unfold like flowers before thee,
Opening to the sun above.[2]

Overcome with a poetic vision of God's providential care for the world, David exults, 'The grasslands ... the hills ... the meadows ... the valleys ... they shout for joy and sing' (Psalm 65:12–13). Although all creation groans in its frustration over the effects of the Fall, a mysterious consciousness of the creative majesty of God still overcomes creation's reticence and calls forth songs of praise (see Romans 8:19–21). I like to think that the birds join that chorus.

This is my Father's world,

And to my listening ears
All nature sings, and round me rings
The music of the spheres.[3]

Even when enemies plot our harm, or trouble dogs our footsteps, David teaches us to find renewed courage through singing of God's glories. Pursued by Saul's men, David composed a song that concludes, 'I will sing of your strength, in the morning I will sing of your love; for you are my fortress, my refuge in times of trouble' (Psalm 59:16).

A mighty fortress is our God,
A bulwark never failing;
Our helper he, amid the flood
Of mortal ills prevailing.[4]

The Scriptures urge us to sing in darkness and pain and trouble and night. Perhaps his habit of singing in prison helped the apostle Paul to pen the joyful and enlightening prison epistles from his cell.

He giveth more grace when the burden grows greater;
He sending more strength when the labours increase.
To added affliction he addeth his mercy
To multiplied trials, his multiplied peace.[5]

The songs we sing around the Lord's Table are especially meaningful.

Jesus, thy blood and righteousness
My beauty are, my glorious dress;
'Midst flaming worlds, in these arrayed,
With joy shall I lift up my head.[6]

Since my singing has been rather circumspect during my lifetime, I trust that there will be much song at my funeral. Morose thought? Hardly. Consider:

Face to face with Christ my Saviour,
Face to face—what will it be,
When with rapture I behold him,
Jesus Christ who died for me?[7]

Or this one:

There's a land that is fairer than day,
And by faith we can see it afar;
For the Father waits over the way
To prepare us a dwelling place there.[8]

I have a feeling that my voice will sound like that of an angel in that land that is fairer than day!

Prayer

Heavenly Father, remind me to look more often in the hymnbook. Such a wealth of uplifting praise, heartening instruction and tender comfort! Blessed Holy Spirit, may the birdsong I hear every morning remind me to lift my heart often in praise and thanksgiving. Amen.

Notes

1 Translated by Edward Caswall from *Katholisches Gesangbuch* (Wurzburg, 1828).
2 Henry Van Dyke.
3 Maltbie D. Babcock.
4 Martin Luther; translated by Frederick H. Hedge.
5 Annie Johnson Flint.
6 Nicolaus L. von Zinzendorf; translated by John Wesley.
7 Carrie E. Breck.
8 Sanford F. Bennett.

september

Changing seasons

Bible reading
Lamentations 3:13–27

As summer eases into autumn, a hint of sadness frames the memories of picnics on the beach. We face the knowledge that the warm summer days are over for another year. Soon we'll be getting out our scarves and gloves. The leaves will fall. The flowers will fade and die.

Of course, there will be no more grass to cut until the spring and no wrestling with weeds. Other work will occupy the time—tuning up the snowblower, hunting for the snow shovel and preparing the flower beds for winter. All this is to be expected. No big deal. Just another changing season in a world of change.

The waxing and waning of the moon. The rise and fall of tides. Clouds spreading and retreating. Sunrise and sunset. Gasoline prices rising. New pop stars. New bulletins on healthy eating.

The mirror also reflects change: wrinkles; receding hairline; more grey hair; squinting; time to make another appointment with the ophthalmologist.

Sometimes the changes come much too quickly: new gadgets to replace ones I haven't figured out yet—DVD players instead of VCRs; MP3s—whatever they are; new computer software; the computer geek at the store telling me that my CD burner is obsolete! He laughs when I protest that my computer is almost new, then winks and points to the latest model. It makes the mind spin.

Change and decay in all around I see;
O thou who changest not, abide with me.[1]

Thankfully, God is changeless. In the midst of Israel's vacillating devotion, God assured Malachi, 'I the LORD do not change. So you, O descendants of Jacob, are not destroyed' (Malachi 3:6). Through his prophet, God reminded Israel that he could be depended upon to reward repentance with forgiveness and blessing. Not a capricious god, Jehovah keeps his promises.

In the New Testament, James warns about being deceived by comparing God with the world around: 'Every good and perfect gift is from above, coming down from the Father of the heavenly lights, who does not change like shifting shadows' (James 1:17). His mercy, his grace, his love and his justice do not ebb! Instead of vacillation, we discover constancy. He is changeless without being immobile; his purposes march forward towards their climax.

God pours his good gifts upon the earth as bountifully today as he has done for millennia. He is the unchanging Father of light, the Giver of every good gift. The everlasting gospel saves as powerfully today as in the days of Paul. And, when God redeems us through Christ, he anchors our destiny to the very throne from which he rules the universe.

Few prophets had to minister in the turmoil through which Jeremiah lived. God commissioned him to pronounce the destruction of Jerusalem and the captivity of the Jewish people. Few prophets endured the persecution he faced. What kept him sane when thrown into a well, fastened in the stocks or lampooned by false prophets? In Lamentations, Jeremiah explains that, although his heart was pierced with sorrow and his stomach full of gall, he trusted in God's love and faithfulness: 'Because of the LORD's great love we are not consumed, for his compassions never fail. They are new every morning; great is your faithfulness' (Lamentations 3:22–23).

Changeless compassion in a world of rebellion and hate; faithfulness in a society of broken promises and discarded treaties; a shepherd and friend whose presence and guidance is as sure today as it has ever been: prayer is as important a means of grace today as it was in the days of Elijah. What a God!

Prayer

Lord, help me not to be so fickle, not to vacillate so much in my devotion to you and in my love for others. Help me to be stable and dependable. And when my moods ebb and flow—for I am human—help me to draw strength from your changeless grace.

When world events and personal circumstances seem to crash and burn, help me to rise like a phoenix from the ashes, lifted into endless hope by your strong arms of love. Amen.

Notes

1 Henry Francis Lyte.

Harvest

Bible reading

Matthew 25:31–46

Harvest is in full swing. Rusty-gold swathes of soy beans, interspersed with vast fields of corn, stretch over hill and dale. Farmer's stands groan under the weight of bushels of tomatoes, baskets of cucumbers, piles of squash, beans, corn and potatoes. Only stubble remains where giant combines rumbled through fields of wheat and oats and barley.

Throughout the Scriptures, God challenges us to bring forth a harvest of righteousness. 'Peacemakers who sow in peace raise a harvest of righteousness' (James 3:18). The book of Hebrews promises a 'harvest of righteousness and peace' (12:11). Paul writes to the Corinthians that God 'will enlarge the harvest of your righteousness', unless they sow sparingly (see 2 Corinthians 9:10,6).

How can we prepare for a harvest of righteousness? Like a farm harvest, a spiritual harvest depends on good soil, good seed, a hard-working farmer and the participation of skilled harvesters.

The good soil, in this analogy, expresses a different lesson from that expressed by the soil in Jesus' parable of the sower. It pictures the need for righteous character. In the Sermon on the Mount, Christ calls us to adopt heart attitudes that prepare us for an abundant harvest: humility, sensitivity to sin, meekness, hunger and thirst for righteousness, compassion, purity of motive, a peacemaking spirit and stamina in the face of persecution. Paul describes the fruit produced by the Spirit in a righteous person as love, joy, peace, patience, gentleness, goodness, faith, meekness and self-control. Both the Beatitudes and the list of fruit of the Spirit define Christlike character. We cannot expect God to reap a good harvest if our characters are warped by pride, impatience and selfishness.

Second, a good spiritual harvest depends on the sowing of the genuine seed of the gospel. Whether or not we have evangelistic skills, all of us can participate in some way in sowing the seed. That involves preparing ourselves with an understanding of the gospel. 'Always be prepared to give an answer to everyone who asks you to give the reason for the hope that you have' (1 Peter 3:15). People who display righteous character, including a hopeful outlook, create curiosity. Curiosity provokes questions. When someone asks us about what we believe or why we react with hope in times of stress, we have an opportunity to plant gospel seed.

Third, a good harvest depends on careful attention to the growing crop. Farmers who expect a good harvest stay close to their fields. They labour long and hard, fertilizing, cultivating and weeding. Believers who long for a harvest of souls stay involved in the lives of their neighbours, friends and acquaintances. Knowing that we often grow weary, Paul encourages us not to give up: 'Let us not become weary in doing good, for at the proper time we will reap a harvest if we do not give up. Therefore, as we have opportunity, let us do good to all people, especially to those who belong to the family of believers' (Galatians 6:9–10).

Paying close attention to the field in which God places us—the people in our lives—leads us to do good whenever we have an opportunity. The kind acts we do enrich our communities, preparing them for a good harvest. These deeds, however, must issue from a humble heart and must not be attempts to impress others with our piety. The parable of the sheep and goats in Matthew 25 commends those who did good without conscious thought. The parable specifically mentions feeding the hungry, clothing the destitute, visiting the sick and imprisoned and showing hospitality to foreigners. But many other activities could also be mentioned. Jesus taught that even offering a cup of cold water is significant in God's sight. We should give especial priority to helping those in the family of God.

Finally, we must remember that, at the harvest, all who participate will reap benefits—not just those with the gift of evangelism, soul winners. 'We have different gifts, according to the grace given us' (Romans 12:6). Some will sow and others will cultivate the soil. Some will water the crop and still others conduct the harvest; 'neither he who plants nor he who waters is anything, but only God, who makes things grow. The man who plants and the man who waters have one purpose, and each will be rewarded according to his own labour. For we are God's fellow workers' (1 Corinthians 3:7–9).

What if our lives produce no harvest? Scattered up and down the country roads lie fields choked by weeds—thistles and goldenrod and vetch and ragweed; fields where no effort was expended. No ploughing; no harrowing; no sowing; no cultivating; no fertilizing: so unlike the fields tended by hard-working farmers. Similarly, and sadly, some will stand before the judgement seat of Christ with no spiritual fruit to offer him.

Prayer
Heavenly Father, I pray that there might be a harvest of righteousness from my life. Strengthen me so that I can labour tirelessly in the field in which you have placed me. Help me to show interest in my neighbours, colleagues, family and friends without being nosey or intrusive. Show me when and how to offer practical and compassionate help. Help me not to be afraid to testify to your grace. Arouse curiosity among my acquaintances that moves them to ask about my faith. Enable me to declare the gospel in understandable and interesting ways. Make my life fruitful. Amen.

Facing a hurricane

Bible reading
Ephesians 6:10–20

In 2005, Hurricane Katrina slammed the US Gulf Coast leaving a trail of devastation in its wake, from New Orleans north through Mississippi and Alabama. People around the world stared in unbelief at TV pictures of a drowned city and miles of flattened homes. Mary Helen and I sat in our dry, comfortable home in Southern Ontario and shook our heads in disbelief. The images seemed surreal: people being rescued from the roofs of their homes, wading waist-deep through putrid water or standing in Gulfport amid the piles of kindling that were all that remained of their homes.

Displaced by the merciless hurricane and its aftermath, hundreds of thousands fled New Orleans to seek refuge as far west as Utah and California. The hurricane also displaced many creatures: dogs, cats, alligators, dolphins and sea birds. Sooty terns and laughing gulls from the Gulf of Mexico were spotted thousands of miles from their nesting grounds—on the shores of Lake Erie and Lake Ontario. Someone even photographed a magnificent frigate bird on the south shore of Lake Erie. Ornithologists tell us that, when captured by the eye of a hurricane and swept so far inland, these strays arrive exhausted after flying many days without food or rest. Unfortunately, the majority die.

While most human evacuees from the Gulf Coast will be able to rebuild their lives, the stress they have gone through is unimaginable and will continue for years to come. These people lost everything: their homes, their cars, their jobs, their bank records, irreplaceable keepsakes. Most of them have to begin again in a new place to rebuild their shattered lives.

Many of us will never experience such a nightmare and yet, from time to time, all of us face spiritual hurricanes, storms that threaten to destroy our foundations. When he described the wise and foolish builders, Jesus referred to this very thing (Luke 6:46–49). The foolish man saw his house swept away in a sudden storm. No wonder Paul exhorted the Ephesians to 'put on the full armour of God, so that when the day of evil comes, you may be able to stand your ground, and after you have done everything, to stand' (Ephesians 6:13).

The 'day of evil' may come as an overwhelming moral temptation, in the grief experienced in the loss of a loved one or through the shattering of a reputation. A plunge into abject poverty or a critical illness exemplifies similar crises. None of us can predict when, or if, an emergency may overtake us. All we can do is ask God to work preparedness into our characters.

Obviously, the US was not prepared for such a catastrophe as Hurricane Katrina. Accusations of corruption and incompetence have arisen ever since. Although no country can adequately prepare for a catastrophe of epic proportions, we can prepare spiritually for the 'day of evil' by putting on the whole armour of God. This involves storing up truth in our hearts and minds for times of despair or doubt. Preparation includes becoming adept at covering our emotional gyrations with the breastplate of righteousness. The more we celebrate God's free gift of justifying peace that comes to us through faith in Christ, the more stable we will become. An appropriation of God's justifying grace can do more than anything else to protect us from the depression, despair and false guilt that haunt so many. No wonder Paul determined to focus more completely on the cross of Christ than all else.

Preparation also involves the daily protection afforded by the shield of faith, having our feet shod with the preparation to share the gospel and gripping firmly the sword of the Spirit through study, meditation and memorization of the Scriptures. To all these pieces of spiritual armour we must add prayer, an indispensable attitude towards God that moves us to bring all our concerns to him.

A sizeable number of Katrina's victims endured because of their faith. Many emerged from the disaster with their focus absorbed by bitter tales of hardship, human failure and expressions of recrimination. Few of these could conceal their anger with authorities and with God. Yet sprinkled throughout the news bulletins were indications that substantial numbers escaped with something more precious than their possessions—their faith and integrity. People such as these were spiritually prepared.

There is no need morbidly to expect disaster to strike us tomorrow. Instead, let's enjoy each day of sunshine that God gives us ... but take some time to put on the whole armour of God. The more adept we become in facing each day dressed in God's armour, the more prepared we will be for whatever comes.

Prayer

Lord, help me to put on the whole armour of God, that I may be able to withstand any sudden storm of temptation. Keep me from being complacent. Help me to be diligent in sinking my roots deeply into the Scriptures through study and application. Amen.

Along the river

Bible reading
Psalm 36

On a golden day one October, when fall colours blazed from hill and dale, we drove east towards Quebec. At a Seaway park, we paused to munch on sandwiches and gaze on the mighty St Lawrence River. Like a toy ship in a bathtub, a huge lake-boat headed downstream towards international markets.

The St Lawrence inspires awe, draining as it does almost a quarter of the North American continent. It was hard to comprehend that the current rippling by me that day contained rain that had fallen on distant Manitoba or Minnesota, and water that had thundered over Niagara's cataract.

Scripture speaks of even greater rivers, the rivers of God: the river that went out of Eden to water the garden (Genesis 2:10); the river of pleasures that God gives his children to drink, a river that abundantly satisfies their thirst (Psalm 36:8); the river that makes glad the city of God (Psalm 46:4); the pure river that flows from the throne of God and the Lamb, along the banks of which grow trees whose leaves are for the healing of the nations (Revelation 22:1–2). God's rivers are inexhaustible, pure, enlivening, enriching—and very mysterious.

The Great Lakes and the St Lawrence Seaway System comprise one of the world's greatest transportation networks. Between the Atlantic Ocean and Duluth, Minnesota, ships traverse a distance of 2,300 miles. The system serves a region that is home to more than 90 million people and where a third of the continent's gross national product is produced. The watershed accounts for forty per cent of US manufacturing and two-thirds of Canada's industrial output.

Yet God's river system is far mightier. Through the instrumentality of the Holy Spirit, his river dispenses grace and mercy to billions worldwide. Under a different image, but one that teaches the same lesson, we read that 'He causes his sun to rise on the evil and the good, and sends rain on the righteous and the unrighteous' (Matthew 5:45).

Love, God's love, makes the world go round. The Lover on High moves men and women to embrace each other in relationships of committed love. The heavenly Father blesses couples with children. And Jesus, who loves children, encourages them to laugh and play. The Almighty causes flowers to bloom and tomatoes to ripen. He plants in hearts an appreciation for beauty and a longing for peace. He inspires acts of compassion and courage.

Like the mighty St Lawrence, the worldwide flow of God's love and mercy doesn't depend on us. We don't deserve it. We can't earn it. We can't stop its flow. It just is—a universal fact of life on this planet. We can reject God's love. We can distort it. We can corrupt it. We can degrade it. We can deny it. But we can't stop it from flowing around us—on and on and on— like the great rivers of earth.

I'm reminded of the symbolism portrayed in the book of Ezekiel. In a vision, the prophet saw water pouring from the threshold of the temple. A messenger from God took Ezekiel by the hand, measured off a thousand cubits and led him through water that was ankle-deep, then knee-deep, then up to the waist. Finally, Ezekiel wrote, 'He measured off another thousand, but now it was a river that I could not cross, because the water had risen and was deep enough to swim in—a river no one could cross' (Ezekiel 47:5). Ezekiel's river was as fathomless as the love and mercy of God.

The apostle Paul prayed for the Ephesians to experience God's boundless love: 'I pray that you, being rooted and established in love, may have power, together with all the saints, to grasp how wide and long and high and deep is the love of God ... that surpasses knowledge—that you may be filled to the measure of all the fullness of God' (Ephesians 3:17–19).

Wherever it flows, God's love exposes sin and promises deliverance from its pernicious power. In the gospel, divine love's most astounding expression, the waters of God's grace wash away our sins and anoint us with the joy of salvation.

Like the water of a great river that we had no hand in creating, God's love for us flows freely into our lives. We depend upon it for life and breath. But the particular love God extends to lost men and women in the offer of salvation can be accepted or rejected. Better to stand on the banks of the St

Lawrence River and deny its benefits than reject God's saving love; wiser to confess the corruption of our hearts; smarter to ask God to wash away the sludge of our sins; far better to reach heavenwards with the feeble fingers of our faith; more prudent to listen to the wooing of the Spirit and invite Jesus into our hearts.

All those who have drunk deeply of the waters of salvation will often gaze in awe at the river of grace that flows from God's presence—much as I gazed at the St Lawrence.

Prayer

Father, Son and Holy Spirit, I shake my head in awe at the uninterrupted flow of your benevolence. In spite of human ignorance and rejection, denial and hatred, you still pour out your blessings on our planet, even on me. I don't understand why you would act this way. But I revel in your love and grace. I celebrate your love! Amen.

october

Remembering sunshine during rainy days

Bible reading
Deuteronomy 8

A summer full of sunshine ushered in an autumn of warm and luminous days—until the clouds appeared. We were near the end of two weeks of travel through Canada's Atlantic provinces. Sunshine sparkled off ocean breakers as we drank in the beauty of Prince Edward Island. Sunshine silhouetted Cape Breton's stunning coastline during our journey along the Cabot Trail. Sunshine poured down as we cooked lunch in a harbour by the shore.

Then, as soon as we arrived in Halifax, the sun began to play hide and seek. Dense fog and drizzle obscured our arrival at Saint John. Two days of solid rain and a week of scattered showers cut short our visit to the flaming hills of New England. Months of warm sunny weather had made us expect more of the same. We felt a little miffed.

Complacency and forgetfulness are such human characteristics! We take our health for granted until it's threatened or lost. We expect God to bless us materially, until unemployment or financial setbacks leave us reeling. Suddenly, the little luxuries we expect become memories. We grumble about the demands of our children until suddenly we stare around at an empty nest. Our free elections bore us until we hear about the struggle to introduce democracy to an autocracy. And what about our salvation? Do we take God's grace for granted?

We have such a tendency to let complacency cool our passions and domesticate our praises that God repeatedly issues warnings: 'Be careful not to forget the covenant of the LORD your God' (Deuteronomy 4:23); 'Does a maiden forget her jewellery, a bride her wedding ornaments? Yet my people have forgotten me, days without number' (Jeremiah 2:32).

In Deuteronomy, Moses' parting series of sermons, he says 'remember' thirteen times and warns Israel not to 'forget' nine times. The wilderness wandering of Israel is a glaring illustration of our human tendency to be selective about what we remember.

The people of Israel kept forgetting that God had led them out of Egypt, parted the Red Sea and provided water from a rock. Their immediate concerns obscured their memory of the Egyptians' cruelty in the slaughter of their male children. They forgot about their labour from dawn to dark making bricks. Yet they did remember the melons they ate.

To offset their tendency to forget, God instituted a series of festivals. The yearly Passover reminded them of their deliverance from the death angel the night before they escaped from Egypt. The Festival of Booths, or Tabernacles, took them back in their memories to the temporary shelters used during the wilderness wanderings. The tabernacle in the centre of the camp spoke daily of the reality of God's presence.

Centuries later, David wrote, '... forget not all his benefits—who forgives all your sins and heals all your diseases, who redeems your life from the pit and crowns you with love and compassion' (Psalm 103:2–4). It's not so serious to forget sunny days during a spell of rainy weather. But we ought not to forget how God has blessed us in the past: our conversion; his leading, protection and presence in difficulties; his provision for our needs; the sins he has forgiven; the sicknesses he has healed.

Having daily devotions is a good way to keep our memories sharp. Reading about the victories and sins of Israel reminds us of the glorious things God can do and warns us about the dangers of rebellion. The Gospels take us back to the amazing ministry and teaching of Christ. The Hebrew song book plunges us into the heart of worship. The book of Acts immerses us in the life and death of men and women committed to gospel proclamation.

The Lord's Supper is a special gift of God. Christ Jesus designed it to remind us of the central role his sacrifice plays in our salvation and ongoing sanctification. Sunday reminds us of his resurrection.

Some denominations lay out the whole church year as an aid to help believers review the broad strokes of redemption: Advent, Ascension, Pentecost and so on. Those of us, like myself, who minister in evangelical churches without this emphasis need to be careful lest we fail to bring before God's people regularly the great themes of the faith.

Although special days are very important, wouldn't it be wonderful if we could make every day special? Wake up with thanksgiving in our hearts? Look around us and give thanks? Look back over our lives—indeed, over redemptive history—and remember all the ways God has led us? Maybe that's what makes some saints so joyful.

Prayer
Blessed Holy Spirit, my memory is selective and flawed. I'm so thankful for your indwelling presence to help me remember. Remind me again of the great themes of Holy Scripture: the creative majesty of God, the inspiration of Scripture and the redemptive acts of Christ. Bring to my mind again the practical ways your grace has followed me all the days of my life. Especially help me to keep the cross of our Lord Jesus Christ central in my thoughts. Without him, I can do nothing. And, on a much lighter note, help me to remember sunshine on rainy days. Amen.

Benevolent autumn art

Bible reading
Psalm 19

Why is autumn—to many of us—the most appealing of the seasons? In northern climes, life in the fall becomes urgent as we store up images for the days ahead. But it's more than that. Hillsides painted overnight with splashes of red, yellow and purple in a thousand subtle shades leave us staring in open-mouthed astonishment.

Trembling aspen crown a far hill with a diadem of gold. The light breeze orchestrates their shimmer into a delicate minuet. Patches of green pine, bronze oak and scarlet maple clothe the hill below the aspen like the robe in a royal pageant. Fingers of hemlock and orderly rows of cedar stitch the robe where it meets the spring-fed valley. Each tree has its own signature— a combination of tint and texture so unique that we can pick out the composition of the forest from miles away.

Mary Helen and I lean against an old fence, and tendrils of pure pleasure link us together in silent homage to the divine artist who crowns the harvest season with such rich abandon. It's a time of year when I don't dare have much film for my camera. Each day seems special, each vista unique, each tree a Byzantine mosaic. Mary Helen has urged me during the autumn to get a grip on my itchy camera-finger. She worries about cupboards overflowing with snapshots. But, as with rainbows and sunsets, moonbeams and snow scenes, words fail when we try to describe the subtlety and drama of autumn. Words certainly failed those scribes who attributed all this to 'Jack Frost' or 'Mother Nature'.

Not much better are those who confidently demythologize creation with their 'scientific explanation' for autumn's palette. They remind us that each leaf is a tiny food factory, in which green chlorophyll acts as a catalyst helping to promote the chemical reactions necessary to transform carbon dioxide and water under sunlight into glucose while releasing oxygen as a by-product. All plants contain pigments that are hidden by the intense green of spring and summer growth. As the days shorten and the nights grow cooler, green chlorophyll gradually disappears.

With chlorophyll gone, leaves can no longer make food. Sunlight reacts on leftover glucose to produce red colours. The leaf colour depends on the degree of sunlight, the amount of glucose left and the variety of other pigments that are most plentiful in the leaf. Xanthophyll is yellow. Carotene shows itself as orange-red. Anthocyanin creates a red and purple effect.

Understanding some of the reasons why the hillsides wear their colours shouldn't lessen the wonder we feel at God's creative skill. Compare his works with those of mankind. People have been polluting the earth with their manufacturing for centuries, while God's leaf factories have been quietly producing food and enriching the earth from the very beginning. And his factories don't pollute, stink, ruin the water table, sting the eyes, destabilize the soil or fill the atmosphere with carbon dioxide. Leaves produce oxygen, not carbon dioxide. Some researchers estimate that one tree purifies as much as forty tons of pollutants in its lifetime!

God is not only a perfect environmental engineer and a peerless manufacturer, but also an astounding artist.

Prayer

O Divine Artist, I bow in worship. I've wondered at Michelangelo's artistry in the Sistine Chapel, but you leave me breathless with praise. Every field; every valley; every country road: all touched by your brush. To think that permeating all your works is not only beauty but also utility and benevolence! Sometimes, Lord, all I can do is stand in awe and shake my head in wonder. Truly, 'You crown the year with your bounty' [Psalm 65:11]. Amen.

Travelling mice

Bible reading
Proverbs 6:6–11

One fall morning, we packed a picnic for a jaunt along country roads flaming with autumn colour. But, when we opened the car door, debris on the seat warned us that something was amiss. In the glove compartment, bits of foil and shards of nut were all that remained of a bag of emergency almonds. Fragments of Kleenex littered the back seat.

Mice had chosen our car for their winter abode! We baited traps with peanut butter and caught a couple of the critters, but by then considerable damage had been done. The heater fan shrieked, then stopped altogether.

At the dealership, the mechanic nodded his head sagely as he warned me about leaving the air intake open. 'In the fall, mice look for a warm place to build a winter nest,' he said. 'What's warmer than a car just returned from a trip to town? Mice crawl into the air intake and build a nest, which often clogs the fan. You've got to make sure you close the air intake every time you come home.'

While I wasn't happy with my repair bill, I had to admire the mice's ingenuity. Mice anticipate the future. Sometimes Christians are not as farsighted, naively choosing to expect God to provide rather than engage in rigorous long-term planning. 'Don't we need to trust God?' they say. Or they argue that Christ may return at any time. 'Of what use will our planning be then?'

On first glance, the Bible backs up these arguments. An abundance of verses urge us to leave the future in God's hands. 'Therefore do not worry about tomorrow, for tomorrow will worry about itself. Each day has enough trouble of its own' (Matthew 6:34).

Remember Jesus' parable about a rich man who laid out careful plans for his future on the basis of an abundant harvest? With the goal of 'taking life easy' for many years, he built barns to store his crop, imagining a future filled with eating, drinking and making merry. God called him a fool. 'This very night your life will be demanded from you. Then who will get what you have prepared for yourself?' (Luke 12:16–21).

On closer inspection, verses such as these don't teach us to ignore planning but rather to include God in all our plans and avoid worry by trusting the future to his care. God encourages us to plan—as long as we add a qualification to all our plans: *If you are willing, Lord, I will do thus and so*. After all, when we plan, we imitate God, the great Planner.

God's creatures, ants as well as mice, have much to teach us about foresight:

Go to the ant, you sluggard;
   consider its ways and be wise! ...
[It] stores its provisions in summer
   and gathers its food at harvest ...
When will you get up from your sleep?
A little sleep, a little slumber,
   a little folding of the hands to rest—
and poverty will come on you like a bandit
   and scarcity like an armed man
(Proverbs 6:6,8–11).

In the parable of the ten virgins, five failed to plan ahead. Their lamps went out because they didn't bring extra oil. Their exclusion from the wedding warns us always to be ready for the return of Christ (Matthew 25:1–13).

In the parable of the talents, the master commended two of his servants who used what he entrusted to them to increase his wealth. The third servant was condemned for doing nothing: 'you should have put my money on deposit with the bankers, so that when I returned I would have received it back with interest' (Matthew 25:27).

Since the future cannot be perfectly predicted, we need to trust God to care for what we cannot prepare for. Yet both parables encourage us to be as prepared as we can be. That means working hard with one eye on all our tomorrows: developing careful budgets, saving for our children's education, planning for our retirements and taking out insurance. It also means maintaining exercise regimens and good eating habits in order to keep our bodies as strong and healthy as possible.

Some people carelessly neglect planning and hard work. Pride leads others to trust in their own ability and ignore God. The balance is difficult to maintain!

As a youthful missionary volunteer, I emphasized trusting God alone to provide all my needs. And God did amazing things. But, looking back, I wonder if I was somewhat presumptuous in my prayers. Perhaps I should have paid more heed to planning and work—especially when Mary Helen and I were married without a penny in the bank. Ah, the naivety of youth!

The pendulum has swung far in the other direction. I admit I could now use more of the adventurous faith I had then. Hence the need for balance. As the Irish ballad goes, 'Put your trust in God, my boys, and keep your powder dry!' Mice have something to teach us after all.

Prayer

Father, help me to live a life that balances planning and hard work with prayer and faith. Guide me in preparing a budget that helps us live within our means. Keep us from debt. Give us wisdom in investing what we have so that we do not become a burden on either society or our children. On the other hand, Lord, overcome my reticence to consider that you may have some unpredictable adventure ahead that requires absolute faith. I submit to you. May your will be done. Amen.

Woodpecker wounds

Bible reading

2 Corinthians 1:3–11

God often ministers peace to my soul during a stroll through the grove of tall trees along our stream. No matter what turmoil threatens the world, the knowledge that these trees have been silently growing for a century grants perspective.

Along the stream, a stand of giant white cedars rises eighty or ninety feet from the rich humus. Recently, I noticed something I hadn't seen before during the two years we've been here. At eye level, they all appeared healthy and strong. But, when I glanced high into the foliage, I was shocked to discover that one of the largest, almost two feet in diameter, was badly wounded. Woodpeckers had chiselled great holes out of the trunk in their search for carpenter ants.

Like trees, people often suffer in ways that are not readily apparent. A personal bout of pain brought this forcibly to my attention.

One day, out of nowhere, the right side of my face seemed to catch fire. I couldn't bear to touch it, and none of the usual painkillers did much to ease the agony. After an initial misdiagnosis, my doctor declared, 'It's not a sinus infection. It's shingles.'

Fortunately, the doctor prescribed an effective painkiller but, even so, agony seldom retreated far below the surface of my consciousness. Thoughts of when I took the last pills and when the next ones were due banished all creativity. Work stopped. Pain took over.

The weeks dragged by, full of questions and interrupted nights. *Why now, when I have important deadlines? Why me? What lesson does God want me to learn? Why won't God answer prayer and take the pain away?* Most often: *How long until the next medication?*

And yet, after the initial eruptions healed, I didn't appear sick. Looking at me, no one would have known how miserable I felt. I was reminded of all the people I had known who lived with pain. *Was I empathetic? Probably not. Perhaps that's the main lesson God wants me to learn,* I mused. *I need to look beneath the surface of life and recognize the prevalence of human suffering. I need to sympathize more readily with those who endure great afflictions.*

My pain lasted for a few weeks. How do some people endure years of pain without becoming bitter, angry and miserable? Amazingly, many saints manifest just such beauty of character, especially my heroes and heroines, the elderly saints whose cheerful greetings hide a history of suffering and loss.

Rare is the eighty-year-old whose smile doesn't hide some pain: failing eyesight; sleepless nights; loss of mobility; angina; arthritis. A glance at the swollen joints on their hands reveals what the smiles on their faces do not. Add emotional hurts to all the physical pain, and I shake my head in admiration at the way their Christlike characters enable them to banish grumbling and bitterness. Some endured years in a troubled marriage. A number have lost a much-loved spouse or child. Yet these heroes exhibit thoughtfulness, kindness and faith. They offer words of encouragement instead of complaints.

Can we develop patience and perseverance without pain? Is the combination of compassion and strength that characterizes Christlike character unavailable to those who don't suffer? Paul writes, ' … we also rejoice in our sufferings, because we know that suffering produces perseverance; perseverance, character; and character, hope' (Romans 5:3–4).

Certainly, empathy is rare in someone who has not suffered. Empathy learned in the crucible of suffering equips us to comfort others. Paul praised the God of all comfort, 'who comforts us in all our troubles, so that we can comfort those in any trouble with the comfort we ourselves have received from God' (2 Corinthians 1:4).

I didn't get many answers to my questions about why and why now. Neither did Job, whose experience was intense beyond my imagination. Perhaps the main lesson lies in learning to trust God in darkness and mystery. The reason why some suffer more than others is known only to God. But I do know that, if God is powerful enough to create and govern the universe, he can overrule our suffering for good. I hope he has done that in my case. In the meantime, I can certainly learn to avoid superficial judgements about others, and I can pray for more empathy with the afflicted.

Prayer

Lord, keep the memory of my pain fresh and real so that I can empathize with others who suffer. Remind me that not all suffering appears on the surface: some is worn on the soul. Hear my prayer. Guide my thoughts and words so that I may offer comfort to those who seek solace. Be with those who suffer with cancer, face the dawn with arthritic joints or struggle with chronic back pain.

Heavenly Father, you endured the loss of your Son. Comfort those who weep for loved ones they have lost and strengthen those whose children have gone astray. Amen.

november

Day and night

Bible reading
Romans 8:28–39

God created a universe full of contrasts. 'And God said, "Let there be light," and there was light. God saw that the light was good, and he separated the light from the darkness. God called the light "day", and the darkness he called "night". And there was evening, and there was morning—the first day' (Genesis 1:3–5).

In the days that followed, God continued to create diverse elements: water as liquid and vapour; seas and dry land; vegetation and animals; fish and birds; man and woman.

These contrasts provide the basis for perspective and definition. A stone is hard, but butter is soft. Fish swim in water, while birds fly in the air. A crow is black, while a cardinal is red. A piece of granite is lifeless, while a coral in the sea houses a living creature.

Understanding and appreciation are blunted where contrast is absent. For example, many people who live in democracies take for granted the freedoms that new immigrants cherish. Long-time residents in lake country or at the seashore rarely appreciate their environment as much as city dwellers who scrimp and save to buy a holiday retreat. Cold drives northern Europeans to vacation along warm, sunny Mediterranean shores.

Does this principle hold true when we consider suffering and sin? A painful bout of shingles near the end of a holiday trip made me think along these lines. Some friends commented, 'What a horrible way to end your trip!' In the normal course of things, I would agree wholeheartedly.

Strangely, however, the agony heightened the enjoyment. The weeks of pain that followed provided perspective, as if the sleepless nights highlighted our vacation enjoyment. How thankful I became that the attack hadn't occurred during the height of our trip! It also strengthened my appreciation for relatively normal health.

Life on earth prepares us to enjoy heaven. In Revelation, John paints a vivid picture of our future as believers: 'Now the dwelling of God is with men, and he will live with them. They will be his people, and God himself will be with them and be their God. He will wipe every tear from their eyes. There will be no more death or mourning or crying or pain, for the old order of things has passed away' (Revelation 21:3–4). But could we enjoy heaven as profoundly without experiencing tears, pain and grief down here?

One of the greatest mysteries of life concerns how God can overrule suffering and iniquity for our good and his glory. God even brings good from the wreckage of our sins by using the sinful experiences to heighten our appreciation of his grace. Remember the incident Luke records in which a sinful woman anointed Jesus' feet with ointment and tears? Simon, the Pharisee in whose house Jesus was being entertained, was indignant at her actions. Jesus asked Simon who would love a moneylender more: one forgiven fifty denarii or one forgiven five hundred. Simon replied, 'I suppose the one who had the bigger debt cancelled' (Luke 7:43). Jesus then pointed to the woman as one who had been forgiven many sins and, as a result, loved much. 'But he who has been forgiven little loves little' (Luke 7:47).

Grace as the undeserved, unearned gift of a merciful God sets apart the Christian faith from all other religions. Many object to grace on two grounds: that it is unjust and that it provides no deterrent to continued sin. But such a view assumes that fear of punishment is the way to deter sin. The apostle Paul had trouble explaining the deterrent power of grace. 'What shall we say then? Shall we go on sinning so that grace may increase? By no means! We died to sin; how can we live in it any longer?' (Romans 6:1–2). It's hard to explain to someone untouched by grace how those who experience Christ's forgiving love inevitably respond to him with love and a new revulsion towards sin. The contrast creates the devotion.

The contrast between living in rebellion against God and being forgiven by God produces profound gratitude and deep devotion. I'm sure that's why Augustine, who was such a depraved sinner in his youth, became such a powerful preacher of the gospel. That's why John Newton, the callous captain of slave ships, when converted, could write 'Amazing Grace'.

Night and day, suffering and good health, depravity and purity: these contrasts heighten our understanding. That explains why some of the most cheerful and thankful people have gone through the deepest waters.

Of course, the effect is not inevitable. We may remember being taught in Sunday school that the same sun that softens butter hardens clay. Sadly, some people become bitter and hard and angry. But, knowing what we know about God's ways, that need not be our experience.

Prayer

Father, I'm learning that we can't expect to go through life without days of darkness and difficulty. In spite of the benefit of affliction, please, Lord, keep me and those I love from as much suffering as possible. But, although as a very human person I shrink from suffering, help me to accept your will when you do introduce it into my life. And enable me, out of the experience, to develop more empathy, understanding and faith. Lord, I know that this knowledge could make me more morose and fearful of the future. Instead, grant me joy in this day of grace which you have given. Amen.

Message of the mountains

Bible reading
Psalm 121

On a train trip through the Canadian Rockies, Mary Helen and I gazed spellbound at rushing rivers, waterfalls and placid lakes. But the jagged mountains especially entranced us. Forests of pine and spruce clothed their lower slopes, thinning out to reveal naked rock rising towards soaring peaks touched with snow. Here and there, a glacier glistened in the sun.

Wherever mountains pierce the sky, they seize our imagination. The Himalayas. The Appalachians. The Alps. Mount Fuji. In Western Canada, the foothills dominate the horizon and draw the eye westwards towards the Rocky Mountains, which rise like spectres out of the grain fields and rangeland of Alberta.

We love every kind of natural scenery: the Boreal forests of Eastern Canada, the coastal islands of North Carolina and even the desert expanses of Pakistan. Mountains, however, add drama to any landscape. They draw the eye up towards heaven itself. During a visit to the gallery of an indigenous artist in British Columbia, I learned that he yearly climbs a mountain for spiritual refreshment. There, high above our human struggles to domesticate nature, he feels close to his Creator.

The psalmist wrote, 'I lift up my eyes to the hills—where does my help come from? My help comes from the LORD, the Maker of heaven and earth' (Psalm 121:1–2). Perhaps the writer had been sleepless and worried about slipping off the pathway of righteousness or being harmed by an enemy: he went on to write, 'He will not let your foot slip—he who watches over you will not slumber; indeed, he who watches over Israel will neither slumber nor sleep' (vv. 3–4). Mountains often figure in the biblical drama as places where God is revealed—Mount Sinai, Mount Zion, the mountain of transfiguration.

No matter how strong we are, we need someone stronger and bigger than us. And when we sleep, we need someone who never sleeps. We need someone who hears our feeble—or frantic—cries for help. But we won't look beyond ourselves and our friends unless we join the psalmist in confessing, 'My help comes from the LORD'—who is bigger even than the mountains.

O. Hallesby, in his classic work *Prayer*, asserts that an attitude of helplessness is essential to prayer. 'Prayer has been ordained only for the helpless ... Your helplessness is your best prayer ... Our helplessness is one continuous appeal to His father-heart.'[1] We often feel most helpless during the struggles we face at the commencement of our Christian life. As time goes on, we often 'slip out of this blessed attitude of helplessness before God. Our former self-conceit and self-sufficiency reassert themselves.'[2]

An admission of helplessness is quite contrary to our nature and upbringing. We've been schooled to be strong, to stand up and take whatever life throws at us. We admire those who are bold and self-reliant. When we face difficulties, we're counselled to 'grin and bear it' and 'keep a stiff upper lip'.

If we're honest, we have to admit that these are forms of social pretence. Even if we're crying inside, we're supposed to put on a brave face. Admittedly, no one likes a whiner, but has our culture taken stoicism too far? In reality, pretending to be what we are not in order to keep up an image that we have it all together is just another manifestation of pride. And pride slams the door on the help God offers.

On the other hand, humility—honesty about how dependent and needy we are—opens the door into God's presence. God loves to answer the prayers of humble, self-confessed helpless children. And few things humble us more than mountains.

Do you feel helpless? Then you're fortunate, for that prepares you for God's help. Perhaps you feel abandoned or misunderstood. You may be racked with unrelieved pain or at the end of your resources. A dream could lie in the dust with every way ahead blocked. Thirty years of marriage may have ended in acrimonious divorce. Your church may have split into factions. Perhaps the actions of a favourite son have left you shocked and grieved. A mountain of bills may mock you. In every situation, the

Scriptures teach us to cry out to God for help. The mountains also remind us that God can do big things—impossible things.

Usually our needs are much less dramatic. They may even appear to be so insignificant that we avoid bothering God with them. But, as our *Father*, God loves to have us talk to him about everything. Nothing is too trivial or too big to share with him.

Prayer includes praise, thanksgiving and confession, but often it is enough to cry, 'Help!'

Prayer

Lord, I come into your presence today crying, 'Help!' You know the burden I bear, the problem I face, the dead end ahead. Hear my prayer from your throne and answer, I pray. Amen.

Notes

1 **O. Hallesby,** *Prayer* (Minneapolis: Augsburg, 1975), pp. 16–18.
2 Ibid, p. 25.

Where the sky springs free

Bible reading
Job 38, especially verses 31–38

When we moved to the country, we began to rediscover the sky—especially the night sky. Arriving home from a meeting or a shopping trip, we like to pause at the door on clear nights to gaze heavenwards. The spectacle of a myriad stars glimmering on the black velvet expanse leaves our mouths hanging open in awe.

A memory of our daughter Debbie when young keeps us from taking stars for granted. Decades ago, when we returned to Toronto after a term abroad, she asked us one night, 'Are there no stars in Canada?'

In Pakistan, we often slept under the stars during the hot season. We would move our string beds up to the flat roof of our house to catch the evening breeze blowing off the desert. As we lay there, gazing at the shimmer of stars against the silky blackness of the night, we felt like royalty selecting diamonds and sapphires for a coronation robe. I'd point out to our three children the Big Dipper, the Milky Way and Orion—exhausting my knowledge, but impressing them.

In the city, a curtain of incandescence veils the stars. Smog smears the indigo of night. Asphalt and steel, and glass and neon, brand land and sky with the scars of mankind's attempts at sovereignty.

Out in the country, the sky springs free: vast; bold; alive; unhurried by the urgency of men and women; unimpressed by the artefacts of centuries of arrogance. The sky proclaims transcendence while it spreads a counterpane upon which human dilemmas shrink to their rightful, Lilliputian proportions. No problem is impossible.

In the night sky, God cracks open the door of heaven to give us a peek behind the veil of his omnipotence. He instils peace and perspective into our frazzled lives. Even Job, the epitome of righteous suffering, found insight when God invited him to look around: 'Can you bind the beautiful Pleiades? Can you loose the cords of Orion? Can you bring forth the constellations in their seasons or lead out the Bear with its cubs? Do you know the laws of the heavens?' (Job 38:31–33). Job's voice echoes down through the centuries: 'I spoke of things I did not understand, things too wonderful for me to know' (42:3).

Ah yes, much too wonderful! With the naked eye, we can see around 5,000 stars. With a common telescope, 2,000,000 come into view. The Hubble Telescope enlarges that vision to billions and billions of stars. In the known universe, there are around 100 billion galaxies and 100 billion stars in each galaxy. The Milky Way galaxy alone has 200 billion stars. Our sun is located in one of the galaxy's spiral arms. One scientist has estimated that there are probably as many stars as grains of sand on all the beaches of the world. The numbers boggle our minds, but not God's. 'He determines the number of the stars and calls them each by name. Great is our Lord and mighty in power; his understanding has no limit' (Psalm 147:4–5).

And what of the distances and sizes involved? A light year is the distance light travels in a year. At a speed of 186,282 miles per second, it covers six trillion miles a year. The Milky Way galaxy, one of billions, is 80,000 light years across. Our sun, fortunately for life on earth, is exactly 93,000,000 miles away, yet it is a small star. Some stars could hold 500 million suns the size of ours. Five of the seven stars in the Big Dipper are members of a relatively near star cluster roughly seventy-five light years away; yet their light takes a human lifespan to reach Earth.

No wonder the psalmists reiterate, '... the heavens are the work of your hands' (Psalm 102:25; see also 104:2; 136:5,9; 8:3; 147:4; 148:3). In the context of this truth, problems, suffering and impossibilities shrink in size. God's nightly display calls us to worship: 'You have set your glory above the heavens' (Psalm 8:1). Yet how carelessly we gloss over the mysterious order and immensity of the heavens! We live and walk and shop and work and love and die beneath the lustre of the stars as if they had no message to herald. We take them for granted when they should leave us breathless with praise.

Prayer

Lord, I worship your omniscience—you know every star by name. You created each one. I stand in awe of your power and skill. All the stars together are but a drop in your heavenly bucket. Lord Jesus, the unimaginable forces that keep the universe in stable motion depend on you, in whom 'all things hold together' [Colossians 1:17]. I bow in wonder at your sovereign power. You are the King of kings and Lord of lords. Infinite Lord, you measure out the unfathomable distances spoken of by astronomers with your fingers. In omniscience, your eyes see the light that streams from stars in the farthest reaches of the universe. You hold the universe in the palm of your hand. All things are yours, and all things exist for your glory. I stand in silent awe. Amen.

Trees for tomorrow

Bible reading
Galatians 6:7–10

I love trees. There's something soothing about walking through an old-growth forest to gaze up at towering maples and oaks. I also love to watch seedlings grow. 'Watch seedlings grow?' you ask. 'Isn't that like watching paint dry?' Not quite.

When we first moved to a country property, Mary Helen discovered something new about my personality. I love grubbing in the mud—if it involves planting tree seedlings. Usually, trees are planted in the spring, but planting in the fall—after tree roots go dormant—is also possible. But why bother to plant tiny seedlings when we may only live on a property for a few years? After all, trees take decades to mature.

Christians face a similar temptation every day: live for the moment or invest in eternity? Our answer to that challenge sets us up for the sceptic's taunt: 'Christianity is all about pie in the sky, by and by.' Well, yes and no.

The Christian faith has a lot to say about living life to its full potential here and now. The Creator calls us to responsible stewardship of the earth *now*. Jesus promises a life of joy and peace *now*. Not a sad, miserable, unhappy life—'I have told you this [about love and obedience to his commands] so that my joy may be in you and that your joy may be complete' (John 15:11). That doesn't sound like a meaningless, frustrating life. 'I have come that they may have life, and have it to the full' (John 10:10).

On the one hand, the Christian life is very *now*-oriented, yet everything we do today reverberates for eternity. Indeed, it is so *future*-oriented that the salvation Christ offers is called *eternal* life: 'whoever believes in him [Christ] shall not perish but have eternal life' (John 3:16).

Energized by hope, the balanced Christian sees beyond the portal of death to heaven itself. The believer looks beyond a world sinking under the weight of unrighteousness to the coming of Christ's kingdom. Justice is ahead. Righteousness will triumph. God's plan will prevail.

With these certainties in mind, we plant seedlings today that will not mature until eternity—seedlings of kindness, gospel witness, service and sacrifice. 'Let us not become weary in doing good, for at the proper time we will reap a harvest if we do not give up. Therefore, as we have opportunity, let us do good to all people, especially to those who belong to the family of believers' (Galatians 6:9–10).

We may or may not see anything come of our efforts. Occasionally, God does give us a glimpse. I remember some missionary colleagues telling me about a poor villager they met years after offering his family hospitality. They were thrilled to learn that their simple act of kindness initiated a successful search for God. The writer of Ecclesiastes exhorts us to 'Cast your bread upon the waters, for after many days you will find it again' (Ecclesiastes 11:1).

Nothing we do out of a sincere motivation to please God will be wasted. The time invested in teaching children in Sunday school will shine like gold. Attention given to young people will sparkle like diamonds. Visits to bedridden seniors will glow far into the future age. Words of witness will glitter with gospel light. Acts of loving service will twinkle like the stars for eternity.

So let's write notes of encouragement; do good in our local communities; visit patients in hospital; invite people home for meals; support missionaries; offer ourselves to usher, play the piano or make coffee; agree to sit on planning committees or serve as deacons; help shingle a widow's roof.

God rewards not only good deeds and caring service, but also sincere sacrifices embraced for his glory. In 2 Corinthians, Paul candidly describes the suffering and persecution he endured during his ministry. In spite of it all, he writes, ' … our light and momentary troubles are achieving for us an eternal glory that far outweighs them all. So we fix our eyes not on what is seen, but on what is unseen. For what is seen is temporary, but what is unseen is eternal' (2 Corinthians 4:17–18). What good advice: to be motivated not by transient concerns but by unseen, eternal realities. So let's cheerfully take up our cross daily and follow Christ.

When I went back to visit the trees I'd planted a decade earlier, I found the weedy field had become a very pleasant grove. How they had grown!

Sometimes we'll see the results of our actions: sometimes we won't. But if we do what is good and right, without worrying about payback, we can be sure that God will be glorified.

Prayer
Heavenly Father, help me to go about sowing seeds of kindness and grace, whether or not I receive thanks or am even noticed. Sanctify whatever I do, that it may contribute to your glory and the coming of your righteous kingdom. Amen.

A November complaint

Bible reading
Psalm 145

I woke to the sound of rain drumming on the roof. Not April showers, not a drought-busting July torrent, but a bone-chilling November deluge. It had already drizzled for three days. My joints ached as I made my way through the chilly house to peer outside at the greyness. *This will not be a good day*, I thought.

It's November. Optimism has fled. Summer days are a memory. The golden garments of autumn lie wet and ugly beneath the naked trees. Winter's snowy gown may soon be woven, but November's drab coat has no ermine fringe.

I brewed coffee and settled down by the window to concentrate on my morning devotions. A couple of verses kept threading through my thoughts: 'Give thanks in all circumstances' (1 Thessalonians 5:18); 'Rejoice in the Lord always' (Philippians 4:4). *In everything give thanks, Lord? Rejoice, on this miserable November day? That seems hardly reasonable.*

In my efforts to rise above the weather, I was reminded that the text calls us to rejoice in the Lord, not in the circumstances. That observation sparked meditation on God's attributes. And, I must admit, pondering God's majesty instead of the weather did lift me into realms of glory:

I will exalt you, my God the King …
Every day I will praise you …
Great is the LORD and most worthy of praise;
 his greatness no one can fathom …
The LORD is gracious and compassionate,
 slow to anger and rich in love.
The LORD is good to all;
 he has compassion on all he has made
(Psalm 145:1–3,8,9).

After my devotions, since it was a Saturday, I headed out to pick up the weekend paper and fill up the car with gas. My trip didn't begin well. At the gas station, as Fred took my credit card, he mumbled, 'Isn't this miserable weather?'

'You can say that again!' I responded before I could catch myself. So much for my resolution to rejoice in the Lord!

It's not easy to look beyond the weather when everyone complains about it—especially in November. In temperate zones, there seems to be a universal animosity towards November. When the novelist Georges Simenon wanted a setting that would depict misery and mystery in the life of a family outside Paris, he chose a rainy November. Indeed, the title he gave to his psychological tale of family horror was—you've guessed it— 'November'![1]

The wipers beat a dirge as I left the gas station. I wondered whether there could be anything attractive in a November landscape. After all, God has left the marks of his creativity and beauty on the whole universe. As the rain began to ease, I looked more closely at the passing scene. Dogwood stems lent splashes of burgundy to the lowlands, where willows radiated yellow warmth. Paper birch supported fans of wine filigree. Red fruit festooned a wild apple tree. Milkweed pods trailed streamers of parachutes.

The landscape projected a beauty I had never seen before. Here and there, evergreens softened the edge of the woodlands where the hardwoods stood exposed. But, instead of seeing a chaotic jumble of branches, I saw them as a gossamer gown clothing the hills.

A row of white pines stood silhouetted against the sky. They all leaned away from the prevailing wind. On the north-west side, their branches were stunted and twisted, while to the south-east, they looked like the bony arms of mothers pleading for their refugee children—or could they be dancers in a ballet?

The earth's physique lay spread out before me. Autumn's vivid wardrobe had been set aside to unveil the undulating beauty of the land. November became a nightgown woven with subtleties of texture and tint invisible until now. The scantily clad earth waited for winter to spread its blanket over the land. Why had I not noticed November's beauty before?

Probably because only praise can draw back the curtain that keeps us from viewing our world from a proper perspective.

Prayer

Lord, I don't really enjoy damp, cold weather, but help me to rise above circumstances—such as the weather—to see things from your perspective. Teach me how to be a more thankful, more worshipful person. Inspire me to rejoice more in who you are— Father, Son and Holy Spirit—and in your amazing works of creation and redemption. Remind me of the futility of grumbling. Amen.

Notes

1 **Georges Simenon,** *November* [Eng. translation of *Novembre*] (New York: Hamilton & Harcourt Brace Jovanovich, 1970).

december

Winter rainbow

Bible reading
Revelation 1:9–20

As we headed for church on a cold, winter Sunday, we saw that our heavenly Artist had been busy again. Overnight, he had transformed our world into a crystal garden. Brilliant sunshine sparkled off the hoar frost clinging to trees and bushes, houses and fields.

Then, rounding the corner at Turkey Hill, we stared in amazement at a phenomenon we had never seen before: a winter rainbow. Shining through a cloud of ice crystals rising from Lake Ontario, the light of the sun created a corona of colour. To the left and right, the colours of the rainbow were intense. In the centre of the arc, it seemed as if two dazzling new suns blazed forth.

Whatever the scientific explanation for this corona of refracted light, the effect was breathtaking. It was as if Christ, who is 'the radiance of God's glory' (Hebrews 1:3), was giving us a preview of his return to claim his bride. In his Revelation, John writes of falling down in worship before Christ, whose 'face was like the sun shining in all its brilliance' (Revelation 1:16). In chapter 4, he describes a rainbow that encircled his throne (4:3).

Years earlier, Ezekiel had written of Christ's glory high above a throne of sapphire:

… a figure like that of a man … he looked like glowing metal, as if full of fire … brilliant light surrounded him. Like the appearance of a rainbow in the clouds on a rainy day, so was the radiance around him.

This was the appearance of the likeness of the glory of the LORD (Ezekiel 1:26–28).

Ezekiel's rainbow signalled the promise and hope that came through the triumph of the Son of God. But a rainbow in a Canadian winter? When the maples stood stark and bare? When the earth was griped in the frigid clutches of ice and snow? When the sun rose late and set early? When north winds rattled the windows?

Our corona was a promise that winter is not the end; it precedes the spring. Beneath the ground, vibrant life waits to spring forth. In the stark maples, sap awaits the stirring that will inevitably come. Slumbering raccoons, chipmunks and bears await the warming sun.

Winter is not a hopeless season: winter is waiting; winter is expectation; winter is the faint light before the dawn, as if even nature stands on tiptoe waiting breathlessly for the coming of the Son of Man.

Meanwhile, many of us face our own personal seasons of winter: dimming eyesight; aches and pains in new places; ebbing strength; more frequent visits to the doctor; tests; cancer; and then that last enemy—death.

Winter is not gloom; it means that hope's harvest is at hand. Christ has plucked the sting from the scorpion of death. We are closer to 'Emmanuel's land', the place where glory dwells; the place where tears are wiped away, where there is no sadness, no pain; the place concerning which Paul wrote, 'No eye has seen, no ear has heard, no mind has conceived what God has prepared for those who love him' (1 Corinthians 2:9). Paul, who ascended to the third heaven to receive unfathomable revelations, understood more than any the astonishing grandeur that awaits all who are saved by the blood of Jesus Christ. For, in that heavenly place, the Lord Jesus Christ shines brighter than any rainbow.

Isaiah writes,

The sun will no more be your light by day,
    nor will the brightness of the moon shine on you,
    for the LORD will be your everlasting light,
    and your God will be your glory.
Your sun will never set again,
    and your moon will wane no more;
    the LORD will be your everlasting light,
    and your days of sorrow will end
(Isaiah 60:19–20).

Rare phenomena, such as our winter rainbow, occur as if the curtain separating heaven from earth is very briefly drawn aside to let a tiny beam of heavenly glory fall on earth. Since the glory of God is more dazzling than the unshielded light from the sun, in our earthly state we dare not see more than an occasional flash. Our fit response to a vision such as Ezekiel, John and Isaiah received is to fall down in worship and then to rise up in hope. A Canadian winter is not really so bad. Ice and snow cannot stop hope from breaking out in praise.

Prayer

Lord Jesus Christ, thank you for this faint glimpse of your glory. I look forward expectantly to that first full glimpse of your luminosity beyond the river. For you are 'the radiance of God's glory and the exact representation of his being' [Hebrews 1:3]. With hope vibrating in my heart, I bow in worship and adoration. Amen.

First snow

Bible reading
Isaiah 1:2–20

The transforming effect of snow on a dull wintry landscape is astounding. Perhaps Mary Helen and I enjoy this season more than some because we spent so many years in the blazing heat of South Asia. Winter finds us looking wistfully through the window for any sign of falling flakes.

Finally, the Snow Maker on High waves his wand. Snow begins to fall. He trims the houses and barns in ermine. He carpets the ditches and fields with white. He frosts the leafless hardwoods and puts Brown and Grey to sleep beneath a blanket of White.

Mary Helen's eyes sparkle as she insists we don parkas and head outdoors. We wander like children through a world transformed. When Mary Helen spies a pine branch loaded with snow, she takes great glee in luring me beneath it so that she can shower me with snow and watch the branch spring free.

Both of us love snow, even though we're not skiers or snowmobilers and Mary Helen struggles to stand upright on icy roads. She grew up in Eastern South Carolina, where a serious snowfall occurs only maybe once a quarter century. On the other hand, snowmen, snow forts, snowball fights and skating on a local creek were part of my childhood. Diverse in our backgrounds, we are one as we cheer, 'Let it snow, let it snow, let it snow!'

Snow—snow—fast-falling snow!
Snow on the housetops—snow in the street,
Snow overhead, and snow under feet,
Snow in the country—snow in the town,
Silently, silently sinking down;

Everywhere, everywhere, fast-falling snow,
Dazzling the eyes with its crystalline glow![1]

Not only is snow much more fun than a cold winter rain, but its effect is also dramatically different. Instead of a soggy landscape full of fog and dripping trees, suddenly everything is covered with a blanket of white down. The rubbish along the road, beer cans and old tyres have vanished. The rusting machinery and abandoned trucks littering a local farmer's yard have disappeared.

No wonder God picked snow as a metaphor to describe his transforming grace: '"Come now, let us reason together," says the LORD. "Though your sins are like scarlet, they shall be as white as snow"' (Isaiah 1:18). The salvation God offers covers our sins by washing away their gory stain and fitting us with a white robe of righteousness.

God's saving grace covers not just minor peccadilloes; in Isaiah, God compares human iniquity to deadly afflictions:

Ah, sinful nation,
    a people loaded with guilt,
    a brood of evildoers,
    children given to corruption!
    They have forsaken the LORD …
    Your whole head is injured,
    your whole heart afflicted.

From the sole of your foot to the top of your head
    there is no soundness—
    only wounds and welts
    and open sores,
    not cleansed or bandaged
    or soothed with oil (1:4–6).

From Genesis to Revelation, the Bible proclaims the astounding message: no matter how terrible our sins, we can be forgiven and changed. The murderer can have his bloody hands washed white as snow. The treacherous wife can become loving and faithful. The coward may become brave. The abusive husband can be made gentle. The selfish workaholic can become thoughtful and compassionate. The addicted teen may find deliverance. The idolater can become a worshipper. The church-wrecker may become a builder.

In reality, every authentic church has in its membership people from these backgrounds. How is this possible? In 1 Corinthians 6, the apostle Paul lists some of those who offend God's law. They include the sexually immoral, idolaters, adulterers, male prostitutes, homosexuals, thieves, the greedy, drunkards, slanderers or swindlers. Then he makes this astounding statement: 'And that is what some of you were. But you were washed, you were sanctified, you were justified in the name of the Lord Jesus Christ and by the Spirit of our God' (vv. 9–11).

Through Jesus Christ, scarlet sinners can become as white as snow: 'for all have sinned and fall short of the glory of God, and are justified freely by his grace through the redemption that came by Christ Jesus. God presented him as a sacrifice of atonement, through faith in his blood' (Romans 3:23–25). God declares unrighteous people righteous—justified—the moment they repent of their iniquities and put their faith in Christ.

Snow may melt away to expose the garbage beneath its covering blanket, but once our trespasses have been covered by the blood of Christ, they are gone. Eternally gone! 'Who is a God like you, who pardons sin and forgives the transgression … ? You … hurl all our iniquities into the depths of the sea' (Micah 7:18–19).

Dear reader, have you confessed your sins to God? If not, I implore you to respond to God's love by repenting of your sins and putting your faith in Jesus' sacrificial death for you. Contact me if I can be of help in explaining the amazing message of the gospel.

Prayer
Lord Jesus, snow reminds me of the astounding way your blood covers my sins. I don't understand why you loved me enough to die for my iniquities, but I accept your cleansing. I rejoice in your forgiveness. I gratefully don the white raiment of your perfect righteousness. I worship you by giving you my heart. Amen.

Notes

1   **Jennie E. Haight,** 'Snow'. Cited in **Robert M. Hamilton** and **Dorothy Shields** (eds.), *The Dictionary of Canadian Quotations and Phrases* (1979; 1982, Toronto: McClelland and Steward Limited), p. 837.

Delayed harvest

Bible reading
Matthew 9:35–38

The first snow has fallen and the cornfield across the stream remains unharvested. There could be many reasons for this delay. Some farmers intentionally harvest their corn later if they plan to turn it into silage for their cattle. Or it could be because of the soggy nature of the fields after weeks of intermittent rain. Perhaps the farmer couldn't get his machinery into the field until frost froze the ground.

Shortage of labour or machinery might be another cause. As a labour-intensive occupation, farming often requires seasonal help. Such has been the case since pioneer times, when neighbours formed harvest gangs to go from farm to farm helping to speed up the harvest. Even today, in our highly mechanized age, combine crews follow the harvests north from the US Midwest into the Canadian prairies. In Southern Ontario, where we live, local strawberry and apple farmers depend on importing labour from Mexico and Central America.

Our neighbour's cornfield might very well illustrate the situation Jesus faced during his ministry. He said to his disciples, 'The harvest is plentiful but the workers are few. Ask the Lord of the harvest, therefore, to send out workers into his harvest field' (Matthew 9:37–38).

In the chapter that follows, Matthew records Jesus' response. Jesus sent out the twelve apostles into surrounding towns and villages with a commission to preach the message of the kingdom. Later, he sent out seventy disciples with a similar task. After his resurrection, he commissioned all his disciples to pick up the gospel scythe so they could participate in the great harvest. He said, ' … go and make disciples of all nations' (Matthew 28:19).

From that day to this, his disciples have witnessed the Holy Spirit reap an amazing harvest. In almost every nation, sinners saved by the blood of Christ gather every Sunday to sing the praises of the Lamb. Obedience to Jesus' missionary mandate has resulted in overwhelming success.

Nevertheless, much remains to be done. Uncounted millions still cry out, 'The harvest is past, the summer has ended, and we are not saved' (Jeremiah 8:20). And almost everywhere we turn the cry goes up, 'The harvest is plentiful but the workers are few.'

At the time of writing, within our denomination alone in Ontario, thirty-five churches are without pastors. Many of these churches have been searching for a shepherd for a year or more. Throughout the Western world there is a serious shortage of young men volunteering for pastoral and preaching ministry. We need to pray for the Lord to call and equip men for pastoral ministry.

For well over a year, a ministry to Afghan refugees appealed, with no success, for men to help teach English. We need to pray for the Lord of the harvest to call men and women to volunteer to use their teaching skills in this unique way. A great open door stands before us in places such as China and Pakistan.

Again and again through the years, a hospital in a Muslim country has appealed for doctors and nurses. Sometimes for a year at a time they have had to shut down their crucial ministry. We need to pray for the Lord of the harvest to call doctors, nurses and technicians to volunteer for overseas service.

An increasing number of short-term teams from Western countries serve in missionary situations. This is an encouraging sign. Unfortunately, at a time when short-term volunteers are increasing, lifelong missionary volunteers are decreasing. True, missionary volunteers from Asia and other non-Western countries have begun to offset this deficit. For the foreseeable future, however, there is a critical shortage of lifelong (career) missionary volunteers from Western countries. The need for church-planters committed to language acquisition and cultural immersion in cross-cultural situations is especially urgent. Let us cry out to the Lord of the harvest to call men and women from our churches to volunteer for lifelong missionary service.

Prayer

Lord Jesus, the harvest is ripe but the labourers are few. I know that you look out on our world and feel enormous compassion.

So many are harassed and helpless, like sheep without a shepherd. Help me to feel your heartbeat. Blessed Saviour, raise up a new generation of godly preachers for our churches. And call men and women to volunteer for lifelong missionary service. Move pastors, teachers, doctors, nurses, technicians and others to hear the call of the lost. And, Lord, if it is your will, please call one or more of our grandchildren into your ministry. Amen.

A crowded Christmas

Bible reading
Matthew 1:18–25

Throughout December, we hear tedious replays of Irving Berlin's *White Christmas*. You know the one: 'I'm dreaming of a white Christmas just like the ones I used to know.' Now, I must admit that I love to wake up Christmas morning to a blanket of white covering field and forest. The arrival of Christmas cards picturing idealized villages deep in snow, kids skating on frozen ponds and sleighs drawn by high-stepping horses creates a certain nostalgia. In our part of the world, we expect a snowy Christmas. Even south in Florida and across the globe in Australia and Fiji, a white Christmas has become part of the mythology of the season.

But some Christmases are green. Temperatures stay well above freezing, balmy enough for some Canadians to play tennis. Maybe that's not a bad thing—reminding us to get back to the real history behind the myth: the story behind the fairy tales of Santa Claus, Frosty the Snowman, Rudolph the Red-Nosed Reindeer; the truth beyond the tinsel and trees, the feasting and buying; the reality beyond the merchandisers who expect to sell more at Christmas than at any other time of the year. Anyone who has tried to find a parking space at a mall during December knows that buying trumps meditation.

The commercialism and crowds surrounding a modern Christmas are very far from the events leading up to the first Christmas. First, there was probably no snow. Second, there were no crowds thronging the manger to worship Christ. God chose only twelve or so people to participate in the original pageant. Most of the relatives and neighbours of Mary and Joseph had no idea what was happening. The religious leaders took no note of the birth of this child until foreign visitors arrived. King Herod and the political establishment missed the event that would separate history into AD and BC time. The innkeepers of Bethlehem were too busy counting their coins to notice another arrival, even if the woman was heavy with child.

Very few had a clue that history would never be the same again. Fifteen months before the birth of Christ, an angel informed Elizabeth and Zechariah that their son John would prepare the way for the coming of the Lord. That makes two who had an inkling. Nine months before Jesus' birth, Mary, and then Joseph, became participants. On the night of his birth, an angel gave the news to two or three shepherds. That makes six or seven. Eight days after his birth, God moved Simeon and Anna to celebrate the arrival of a Saviour. That makes eight or nine included in the drama. Almost a year later, the Magi arrived. Although the text does not specify that there were three wise men, we know there must have been at least two. If we add up all the participants, we find that God specifically chose eleven or twelve people to take part in the most astounding event in history—the incarnation of the Son of God.

Why so few? These twelve had something in common. Although quite a young woman, Mary's words reflect a wisdom beyond her years. She said, 'My soul glorifies the Lord and my spirit rejoices in God my Saviour' (Luke 1:46–47). Joseph 'was a righteous man' who did not want to expose Mary 'to public disgrace' (Matthew 1:19). Elizabeth and Zechariah 'were upright in the sight of God, observing all the Lord's commandments and regulations blamelessly' (Luke 1:6). Simeon 'was righteous and devout' (Luke 2:25–26). Anna 'worshipped night and day' (Luke 2:37). The text reveals nothing about the character or habits of the shepherds. However, the speed with which they went to find the baby and the way they left 'glorifying and praising God' (Luke 2:20) leads me to believe that they were very sensitive to God. The Magi undertook a lengthy and dangerous journey with the express purpose of worshipping Christ (Matthew 2:2).

These twelve participants are linked by their spiritual sensitivity. They were conscientious worshippers—devout seekers after God.

In his Sermon on the Mount, Christ taught, 'Blessed are the pure in heart, for they will see God' (Matthew 5:8). Martyn Lloyd-Jones pointed out that the purity mentioned here denotes singleness of vision and freedom from defilement. By singleness of vision he meant a focus on God—a God-centredness. This clear vision of God leads the pure in heart to embrace what is good, true and holy—to flee defilement of any kind. In the grubby world in which we live, such purity is rare. Those who treasure such purity see beyond the tinsel and trappings of Christmas—they see God.

Prayer

Father, purify my heart, that I may feel again some of the wonder of the incarnation. Cleanse me from any defilement. Lord, I know you are not a cosmic killjoy out to spoil our celebrations, but please help me to keep from being distracted by all the holiday static that drowns out the true music of Christmas. Amen.

Tracks in the snow

Bible reading
Ephesians 4:17–5:2

One morning, I woke up to discover that an inch or two of light snow had covered everything in a fleecy blanket of white. For almost a week after that, I walked the trail along the back of our property, looking for tracks.

The first day, I could trace where rabbits had scampered through the snow. The abundance of tracks warned me that it would be a hard winter on the plants they gnaw for food when the grass disappears. Squirrels had also left the sign of their passing.

The second day, several strange new tracks appeared. I'm sure one belonged to a raccoon. The other probably marked the meanderings of a vole. The third day, I was excited to see that ruffled grouse had visited the sumach grove looking for food. Down the country road near the woods, signs showed the passing of a sizeable herd of deer.

Those familiar with the lore of the woods can identify each animal and bird by the tracks they leave. Similarly, our lives leave the impression of our passing on the lives we touch. Paul wrote to Timothy urging him to 'set an example for the believers in speech, in life, in love, in faith and in purity' (1 Timothy 4:12). Paul could call Timothy to an exemplary life because he personally had chosen to follow Christ so completely that he could say, 'For to me, to live is Christ and to die is gain' (Philippians 1:21). The great apostle's life was so transparently holy that he commended himself 'to every man's conscience in the sight of God' (2 Corinthians 4:2) and asked the brothers and sisters to 'follow our example' (2 Thessalonians 3:7), since '[we] make ourselves a model for you to follow' (2 Thessalonians 3:9).

Of course, perfection cannot be found in any human hero. Paul admitted, 'I know that nothing good lives in me, that is, in my sinful nature' (Romans 7:18). We would be wise to heed Peter, who reminded us that only Christ Jesus left us the perfect example, 'that you should follow in his steps' (1 Peter 2:21). Yet we learn much from other believers.

One of the great values of Scripture is the inspired portraits it paints of patriarchs and prophets, kings and shepherds, who left their marks on redemptive history. In some cases, the story gleams with light; in others, the malevolent glow of brimstone warns us away from the pathway to destruction. There we discover Adam and Cain, Abraham and Jacob, Rachel and Ruth, Hezekiah and Manasseh, Saul and David, Judas and Paul.

Even depraved lives are recorded, 'as examples to keep us from setting our hearts on evil things as they did' (1 Corinthians 10:6). Esau sold his birthright for a quick meal. Like unhappy taxpayers, the Israelites grumbled under every palm tree. And like corrupt executives salting away millions, King Solomon hoarded gold and horses and wives.

The tracks left by godly men and women, however, are what inspire us to climb the upward path. 'By faith Abel offered God a better sacrifice than Cain did … By faith Noah, when warned about things not yet seen, in holy fear built an ark to save his family. By faith Abraham … made his home in the promised land … [and] offered Isaac as a sacrifice' (Hebrews 11:4,7–9,17).

Besides biblical biographies, God often uses more contemporary stories of godly men and women to challenge us to walk more carefully in the footsteps of Jesus. The cross-centred ministry of L. E. Maxwell, the gospel energy of John Wesley and the astounding mind of C. S. Lewis have recently inspired me to greater heights.

But it's not only spiritual giants who leave a mark. All of us can point to the tracks left by those who blessed our lives. I remember Florence Scruton's example of cheerful thankfulness in spite of declining health, Elaine Mutter's generosity during our mission years and the enthusiasm for the gospel exhibited by Pakistani pastor Hidayat.

Sadly, I can think of others who have left behind an example of schism, controversy or moral bankruptcy. So I need to ask myself: What tracks do I leave? How deep is my devotion to Christ?

Prayer

Lord, help me to follow in the footsteps of your Son. May my life not be a cause for others to stumble but instead a reflection of the light that streams from your presence. Keep me from leaving behind a memory of complaints and stubbornness, of bitterness or anger, of gossip and stinginess. May my neighbours, children and grandchildren see a godly life characterized by perseverance in pain, victory in temptation, consistency in devotions, humility in service and compassion towards others. Clearly, Lord, I need the help of your Holy Spirit today—every day. Amen.

About Day One:

Day One's threefold commitment:

- To be faithful to the Bible, God's inerrant, infallible Word;
- To be relevant to our modern generation;
- To be excellent in our publication standards.

I continue to be thankful for the publications of Day One. They are biblical; they have sound theology; and they are relative to the issues at hand. The material is condensed and manageable while, at the same time, being complete—a challenging balance to find. We are happy in our ministry to make use of these excellent publications.

JOHN MACARTHUR, PASTOR-TEACHER, GRACE COMMUNITY CHURCH, CALIFORNIA

It is a great encouragement to see Day One making such excellent progress. Their publications are always biblical, accessible and attractively produced, with no compromise on quality. Long may their progress continue and increase!

JOHN BLANCHARD, AUTHOR, EVANGELIST AND APOLOGIST

Visit our web site for more information and to request a free catalogue of our books.

www.dayone.co.uk

Rainbows and Promises
Fifty-two readings from the Bible with
selections from well-loved hymns

JEAN WILD

112PP, ILLUSTRATED PAPERBACK

ISBN: 978–1–84625–098–9

Come for a stroll and a chat down 'Memory Lane' and find rainbows of blessing and promises of encouragement along the way. We'll rediscover plenty of memories of days long gone, some to bring smiles and some, maybe, a few tears. All, however, can bring an insight into the special love, care and concern that God has for each of his 'children' of fifty-plus years. So, leaving any regrets behind, let's head towards the everlasting adventure that's waiting for all who are willing to go arm in arm together. Won't you join us as we travel along the pathway that leads to the golden future waiting beyond the sunset?

Born in Bury, Lancashire, Jean was a self-employed shopkeeper for some years. Conversion in 1963 began her lifelong love of the Scriptures. Jean's love and concern for people is evident in her choice of secular and Christian work. Over the years her occupations have included office work in customer relations, being a doctors' receptionist, an Age Concern Volunteer, 'Activities Organizer' in a residential home, and work in Senior Citizen Outreach. Throughout her busy life, she has made many friends, keeping her Lancashire sense of humour. She loves to laugh and often sees the funny side of human nature. Jean's husband, Stanley, died in 1996. She has two sons who are both married with Christian families.

This book came to me at just the right moment—a month after I turned 65! How great are the reminders Jean gives us for the 'third age' of our lives—to ask the Lord to 'speak in the stillness', to remember that 'God holds the key of all unknown', that 'Jesus knows our every weakness', that we are to continue to 'run the straight race', that 'When morning gilds the skies' we can say 'May Jesus Christ be praised'.
JOHN GOLDINGAY, PROFESSOR OF OLD TESTAMENT, FULLER THEOLOGICAL SEMINARY, AND ASSOCIATE RECTOR, ST BARNABAS CHURCH, PASADENA